Wakefield Press

The Bridge Builder

Beverley Rybarz worked as confidential secretary to
the District Commissioner of Papua New Guinea in the
1950s. In Australia she has been an executive secretary
for a number of organisations. Beverley is now
enjoying her retirement in Adelaide.

The Bridge Builder

BEVERLEY RYBARZ

Wakefield
Press

Wakefield Press
1 The Parade West
Kent Town
South Australia 5067
www.wakefieldpress.com.au

First published 2005
Copyright © Beverley Rybarz, 2005

This story is based on fact but due to the fallibility of memory, may not be
entirely accurate.

Edited by Julia Beaven
Cover designed by Liz Nicholson, designBITE
Text designed and typeset by Clinton Ellicott, Wakefield Press
Printed and bound by Hyde Park Press

National Library of Australia
Cataloguing-in-publication entry

Rybarz, Beverley.
The bridge builder.

ISBN 1 86254 634 7.

I. Title.

A823.4

Dedicated to

My daughter Jane
To quote Stan: 'We did good here'.

The five freedoms

To See and Hear
What is here,
Instead of what should be,
Was or will be.

To Say
What one feels and thinks
Instead of what one should.

To Feel
What one feels,
Instead of what one ought.

To Ask
For what one wants,
Instead of always waiting
For permission.

To take Risks
In one's own behalf,
Instead of choosing to be
Only 'secure'
And not rocking the boat

Virginia Satir

Contents

Prologue

'I like the one holding his cock the best.' I can remember giggling nervously and sneaking a peak to see who had made such a bold remark for those days. And there she was, a gorgeous blonde girl with a laughing audacious face and daring green eyes; a delightful creature with an Irish voice like a song. Her name was Sheila and we were at the Hotel Cecil in Lae, New Guinea, looking at a painting of cock-fighting birds in an Indonesian art exhibition.

The hotel was owned by a warmhearted woman called Ma Stuart who encouraged the community of 600 white residents to have pride and involvement in the beautiful tropical town of Lae. This helped us all cope with our primitive living arrangements, the limited diet and lack of entertainment. As a gesture to the Lae community she had sponsored this exhibition.

I stood out like a sore toe, obviously ill at ease, with a peachy-pink complexion advertising that I had just arrived in New Guinea and hadn't started turning the malarial yellow. I was also unsuitably dressed in a voluminous floral garden-party frock under which my skin laboured with prickly heat. Lae seemed to me like the last outpost of the British Empire; all Queen and Country. Well-trained *haus bois* clanged dinner gongs, threw open the more-often-than-not-imaginary double doors and advised dinner was

Hotel Cecil, Lae

served. Resplendently dressed in embroidered *laplaps* they proudly vied for the title of 'number one *haus boi*'. It was difficult to take all this seriously, especially while living in a glorified tin shed.

This was my first formal outing and I was immediately drawn to Sheila who was restlessly moving around the bar area and constantly looking at the door.

Suddenly she groaned, 'Oh fuck here he comes!'

For no reason at all, my lungs seemed to cease functioning, my legs wobbled uncontrollably, my body trembled and I felt as though the soaring of my heart lifted me off my feet. Standing in the doorway was the most arrogant, strikingly handsome man I had ever seen. He was dressed in hugging white sharkskin pants, his white shirt was open to the waist and a sharkstooth necklace shone on tanned flawless skin. He had blond hair and slanting blue eyes with long lashes and effectively dropped lids. With a diabolical smile, his eyes rested on my face and gradually moved over my body. I felt hot and naked. I was shaking so much I had to hold on to a chair.

I didn't know it then, but this was the beginning of my adventure of a lifetime.

Part 1

1

In the beginning

I came from an adventurous and diverse family. My mother was born from English (Salvation Army) and French parentage and my father from English aristocracy and Welsh lineage.

Grandfather Rowley pompously believed God had chosen him to save the Aboriginal people in Australia, so leaving Chester, England, he became a Brigadier in the Salvation Army to do just that. He married Salvationist Captain Florrie Judd, had five disparate children and lived all over Australia and New Zealand, eventually settling in Adelaide and running a successful building business.

One son Frederick settled in America and became a builder and a composer of music. Three cousins come to mind from the American connection; June Rowley and her husband Bud Hough, and actress Jean Peters who was married to Howard Hughes for 15 years then married Bud's brother, Stan Hough, a producer and director for 20th Century Fox Films and CBS News.

Son William settled in Tahiti. He was deported twice but returned and married a 15-year-old Tahitian girl and founded a dynasty of property and wealth. His wife died, the two Tahitian daughters married Frenchmen and settled in Paris and the sons eventually expanded his business. Much later William married a German-Australian girl.

One daughter (my mother), a superb exponent of Chopin, became a school and music teacher and thanks to the Salvation Army, another son, Harold, played in a jazz band, and William eventually played in the Adelaide Symphony Orchestra.

Other members of this family included a baker, an architect, an Australian Army Brigadier, an opera singer, a seamstress, a tailor, a restaurateur in Canada, a logger in the Philippines and several happy alcoholics.

Grandmother Bickford left her titled family and eloped with a Welsh sea captain, Captain Owen-Owen and had three sons, one of whom was my father Richard. From this elopement an English Poet Laureate, a ship builder, an English politican, an author, an inventor and a maker of fruit cordial joined the family.

The Captain died at sea and as Grandmother's only claim to fame was writing poetry this beautiful woman allowed certain gentlemen to support her resulting in varying living standards and an inordinate number of children.

My dad from the age of nine to 13 worked for a pastoralist family. With one Aborigine he drove cattle from Northern Australia to Adelaide to help support his mother. He was one of the first advocates of reconciliation for the Aboriginals. He became a successful broker and he and my mother had a loving, happy marriage.

Offspring from these unions travelled the world and settled in 10 countries, each being a 'bridge builder' in their own way.

2

Growing up in Adelaide

What are my memories of growing up in Adelaide? I recall ugly houses, religion, pleasant trams, discipline, cleanliness, family values, quality before quantity, ignorance and abstinence.

The first eight happy and unspoilt years were spent at Westbourne Park during the 1930s. Our treat as kids was a halfpenny a week pocket money for the 'ha'penny tray' which we would hoard to swap with our friends. Occasionally I yearn for a ha'penny lolly, a kali sucker, or aniseed ball, the piece of that special-tasting fritz the butchers gave us and the versatile 'Rawleigh's Ready Relief' man who worked house to house selling everything from soap to foul-smelling mustard rubs.

We were allowed to see a film occasionally providing it was a suitable Walt Disney. We played hopscotch, read books, and on Sunday nights we listened to the Lux Radio Theatre on the wireless. If we behaved well, we were permitted to listen to the 'Dossier on Demetrious', 'Shadow of Fu Man Chu' and 'Deadly Nightshade' during the school week. We always had a roast dinner for Sunday lunch, with cold meat and salad, scones, jam and cream for tea, and school friends were often asked to share the meal. This was our simple life.

The milkman carried the big pails of milk on an extraordinary bicycle contraption, and he yodelled as he poured the milk into our billies hanging on the fence. We could hear the *Bottle-O* yelling from the top of the street, clumping along with his old horse and buggy: 'Any empties – get your empties?' And then he would count each bottle and pay Mother according to the type and size. Our mothers chose the hot bread from the baker's truck, and the vegetable man from his green truck would also sell eggs and fish and rabbits – two for threepence.

We kids belonged to Sunday schools and church groups, Protestant and Catholic, and there were strong divisions between the two. Protestant men were very often Freemasons, my father for one, and Catholics considered they were the devil's messengers as Freemasonry was a secret society. The Protestants thought the Catholic Church had too much power and kept their flock poor and ignorant. Catholics seemed to work for the Public Service, controlled the unions and hated the British. Protestants appeared to have more money, less children and hated the Irish. This dislike was fostered at the schools by the Irish Catholic priests and carried on by parents, usually of Irish background. The Protestants were equally guilty, and with that Freemason background there was a strong anti-Catholic atmosphere in the home. Mixed marriages were taboo and invariably ended disastrously unless one partner changed religion. We kids carried on a feud we neither understood nor cared about.

We caught buses and trams, or rode bikes. Parents did not drive kids anywhere. If a child showed any potential on stage or dancing it was immediately stifled if the child came from a 'nice family'; only 'common people' performed. It was considered pushy and showing off and those who did perform were not encouraged to visit.

Swearing was not known – I can remember being sent to my room for saying that my aunt, who looked lovely in white linen on a hot day, had 'sex appeal' – I had no idea what it meant. Another time I asked my father what 'fucking' meant and was sent to my room again. As usual no explanation was forthcoming. I had to wait until I was 19 years of age to learn about that. However, we were happy, healthy kids without guile and considered our life nearly perfect.

Heat-wave nights were spent on front lawns – we would sleep in the knowledge it was safe. We could walk and play in parks, beaches, creeks without worry and cars were left unlocked, bikes unchained on verandahs or in front of shops, and milk money left out. We did not hear of children being molested. Our parents were caring and sincere. There was rarely money to spare even though Dad was on five pounds a week during the depression and that was considered reasonably good. Any unspent money was cautiously banked.

Men respected women. They raised their hats in welcome, opened doors and stood up when women entered a room. They gave up their seats on trams and buses and always, always paid for any outings, lunches, shows, and drinks. Boys and young girls were expected to give up their seats in buses and trams for elderly people, pregnant women and mothers with small children, and could be reported to school if they did not.

Women were not allowed in front bars, and were frowned upon if seen in a hotel lounge. Women were cherished and to be seen drinking or to swear in their presence was a terrible thing.

There were no vacuum cleaners so rugs were hung up on the line and beaten. Clothes were damped down, rolled up and then ironed. Even outside taps were polished. Velvet soap was cut into little pieces and used in the copper for boiling the clothes, prior to them being hand wrung, blued with Reckitts Blue, then rinsed. Washday was always on Monday and took all day. Eventually we did have Rinso, Persil and Oxysuds but the detachable collars on men's shirts were always scrubbed first with Velvet and then starched. There was thick starch for the collars and then thinned starch for the shirts and linens. After the washing was completed, the kitchen, toilet and laundry floors were scrubbed using the copper water. The end result of these labours was a very grumpy mother on Monday night.

We used ice chests and the iceman called a couple of times a week – and things were grim if we forgot to empty the drip tray. Many families had outside toilets with cut up newspaper for toilet paper. We had to save little pieces of wood so we could fire up the chip heater for showers or baths.

We had dedicated teachers with authority; they used the cane when considered necessary and gave us 'lines' – a punishment for being naughty. Oh the boredom of writing the same thing over and over. Nurses were well trained on the job, discipline was extreme but there were no cross infections, and never any strikes. The word of the doctors and the matron was law.

I was eventually sent to a private school run by English Anglican Sisters not known for their worldly knowledge. We had the St Barnabus boys training for the Anglican priesthood next door and one of the boys proudly displayed his dickie through the fence when I was playing tennis. I had a good look (the first I'd seen) and then of course told Dad over dinner that night – I thought he was going to faint! I was in big trouble with the Sisters anyway for leaving school without permission the previous week but it appeared I was to be forgiven for that indiscretion if this last little matter could be resolved 'sensibly'. The sisters told me we should all pray a lot!

Fortunately St Peter's Day was looming which meant we would get special treatment from 'above' so all our sins would be forgiven. St Peter's Day for us meant a special service at St Peter's Cathedral with all the Church of England schools present. This was ostensibly to celebrate St Peter saying, 'Upon this rock I will build my Church'. We were not told what King Henry VIII got up to so we didn't understand why the Catholics became upset, that having broken away from their church all that time ago we also pinched their saint for ourselves.

The service was impressive because of the magnificent sound of hundreds of young harmonising voices in a large cathedral. The Bishop confirmed some of us and everyone took bulging envelopes of saved pocket money as a contribution to the welfare of our black brothers. These matters were taken seriously and the traditions became important to us all. Religion played a large part in our lives, and sin meant hell.

Also impressive was that we had a half-day off on St Peter's Day and we would meet the young men after the service, one of whom could well be the husband of the future.

By the time I was about 13 my life had taken an interesting turn. My family moved to Somerton Beach. Don Moore, Bob Brown, Bill Brooks, Len Thompson, Dick Fidock and Elliot Shae started flirting with me over our front fence and took me skating: knee knocking stuff! I'd had my sex education talk from Mum, 'You don't let a boy's hand go up your skirt or down your chest!' – so I was well equipped to cope with any emergency. I recall wondering about some of the lads' strange behaviour when I was cuddling and feeling pressures that dear Mother had not explained at all! Reminiscing hundreds of years later with an old school friend, he told me how he used to cycle down from Kensington to Glenelg to see me, but had to painfully walk all the way home pushing his bike! We had it made. Why did the feminists change it all?

I was allowed to go to the Saturday afternoon matinees by this time – threepence to go in and threepence to spend. *The Green*

Dragon, *The Phantom* and *Buck Rogers* were the serials – what an intellectual talking point they were until the next week. Of course we didn't have lipsticks, hairstyles, nail polishes, fashion or pop songs to talk about. However we did have necking in the back seat of the theatre. That's why we had to get there early, to get the most private seats.

Our parents warned us about 'touching ourselves.' This could send us blind or, probably worse, totally insane. I can tell you it turned us off it a bit and wanking was temporarily abandoned!

Living at the Bay, we spent hours on the beach, some well-to-do kids yachting and we poorer ones, canoeing. Our other passion was roller-skating. Glenelg Bay during the 1940s was almost cosmopolitan – there were Chinese people and sometimes groups of Aborigines would walk along the beach, keeping to themselves. I always felt they looked sad and wanted to talk to them, wondering whether they knew my grandfather, the Brigadier, but Mother said I shouldn't get 'chatty with people who were different.' I didn't actually meet an Aborigine until I was 34 years of age.

I started to enjoy school more. To get there I caught a tram from Glenelg and another tram from the Gresham Corner. There we would congregate, making arrangements for after school. Such dens of iniquity as the Devon Milk Bar were very popular. There was also the sophisticated activity of collecting packets of Craven A, XXX, Ardath, and Capstan cigarettes. These were rationed due to the war and although most of us 'didn't inhale' we became addicted fairly quickly.

By this time, I was allowed to go to well-run church dances. Our mums would usually make our evening dresses, appropriately modest of course, but we would have chores to do to earn them. Mine was polishing the doorsteps, dusting the Dresden china and cleaning those outside brass taps. We played a great deal of sport. We girls played tennis, basketball and hockey, and the boys played tennis, cricket and football, with our parents supporting our interests. They too were usually keen tennis players and enjoyed their contract bridge evenings. They had member's tickets to Adelaide Oval and we teenagers went with them just to flirt and gossip.

The social event of the year was either the *Blue and White*, the Saint Peter's school dance, or the *Red and White*, the Prince Alfred school dance. We would just about sell our souls for an invitation in the post, with the school emblem on the front, and the tantalising little program where dances were booked in advance; *Gone with the Wind* had nothing on us. The boys wore the school blazer and the girls their special gowns. A prefect escorted his partner wearing a white blazer and the lucky girl would be so overbearing and conceited everyone would hate her.

We were encouraged, firstly by our school and then our parents, to do volunteer work. Many hours were spent in hospitals wrapping bandages, selling badges for charity or picking and selling daffodils. It was considered to be the right thing to do and we never questioned it.

Everything revolved around family; parents were totally in control. Mothers rarely worked and their time was spent keeping everything spotlessly clean. Rarely precocious, we were secure, well-mannered children with supportive parents. We girls had sewing lessons, and learnt to cook from our mothers, so we would be well equipped for marriage when the time came. Embroidery was also encouraged, so that we would have a full 'glory box' of appropriate linen. I never did find out about that 'glory!' The boys with their dads learnt how to fix things, make things and understand the wonders of electricity and bicycles and noisy engines. We all had a bank savings account at school and money was put away from a very early age. Credit cards did not exist.

I schooled until Leaving standard. More boys than girls reached the next level, Leaving Honours, qualifying them for university. Girls were not encouraged because the only job they seemed to get with an Arts Degree was air-hostessing, and this was dependent on a fluency in languages. Those attending university had to pay for the privilege. Scholarships were only awarded to the very bright. Students lived at home for the duration of the course and there was no government assistance. There was a dominance of men in the sciences and women in arts and there were technical schools for those who wanted a trade, or who lacked higher education abilities.

The rest of us went to work, many aged 15, some in trades, the others as clerks or salespeople. The system worked; the University got the best quality graduates and the rest of us worked without question, changing our job when we got bored. There were plenty of jobs! Most men, the breadwinners as they were called, worked for 50 years, sometimes without changing jobs.

I spent a year of secretarial training at Miss Mann's Business College. Because Miss Mann thought I was a bimbo and was sure I would not pass her 4 subjects, I restudied three General Leaving subjects on my own at home, passing them with Honours. Passing seven subjects of this calibre was unheard of and it was pleasing to note Miss Mann's sour expression when I did. Subsequently these subjects were brought into the curriculum.

My first relieving job was at the GPO and I was the only Protestant amongst the Catholics. As mentioned previously, the Public Service was predominantly Irish Catholic and I was very apprehensive about this. Actually they weren't too keen about me, such was the dislike between these religious factions. It was easy to get jobs just after the war. My weekly wage was 17/3d, ($1.80), out of which went eight shillings (80 cents) board to my mother. I then paid for bus fares, lunches and clothes with the rest.

We had one wireless at home and a record player. We teenagers drooled over Nat King Cole, and songs like *Mona Lisa*, *Give Me a Kiss to Build a Dream On* and *Tenderly* were sung with great pathos. *In the Mood* sent us into a frenzied jitterbug.

We saved and borrowed from parents to go on the Gulf Trip; a 'without parents' trip up the gulf for a week sailing on either the *Minnipa* or *Moonta*. Tubs would probably better describe the ships but we adored it.

Everyone we knew seemed to be on board. We all flirted with the officers and heavy necked and drank mint juleps and gin slings with the boys we knew, and occasionally a girl would get pregnant and be sent to an Anglican home in New Zealand. She would be worked hard scrubbing floors and piles of laundry until the birth of a baby she was not permitted to see before adoption. An illegitimate child was considered a disgrace. If one broke the rules, society was harshly critical.

When I was 18, I transferred to a reasonable job at the Electricity Trust, which was considered on a par with a bank job. Unfortunately my mother wouldn't let me take a trainee journalist position at the *Advertiser* which the editor had offered me. Mother did not believe I was mature enough to handle the night work involved; she was probably right but I was furious.

We were ignorant and suspicious of foreign places other than England and cultures other than our own. When war was declared we were loyal to England and went to fight without question. We were virgins forever and were contented but naïve. We knew nothing about Aborigines but firmly believed that they were well cared for by the Church and the Missions, and that as long as we gave our spare money generously to our visiting Bishop, the Aborigines would luckily end up just like us, hygienically clean and well fed.

A good block of land could be bought for 200 to 300 pounds and a house built for around 4000 pounds. So this is what happened – we married early, built the house and had the children. Well, that's what most people did. I didn't, as you will see as this tale progresses.

One of the best memories for many of us was the family holidays to Yorke Peninsula or Port Lincoln or Victor Harbor. The car, with a trailer on the back, was packed days before departure with a pressure kerosene stove (a metal box with a large hole at the bottom to go over the burner and holes in the top to act as a breather), a small icebox and enormous quantities of water contained in a water carrier on the front of the car. We added bags of flour, sugar, potatoes, onions, and quantities of tinned food and a large round bowl for washing dishes and possibly clothes. Two empty barrels and a piece of wood to erect a toilet were important as was chicken wire to make a coop for the chooks. Yes, they went too, with the cat and dog, and the Red Cross box for the accidents that would probably occur, the fishing rods, the nets for crayfish and a massive fold up tent. I don't know what was more exciting, the packing up or the arrival at the destination.

I can still see the dozens of crayfish our fathers cooked for our evening meals and the 'no limits' salmon trout our mothers deep-batter fried in dripping. Every couple of days ice, bread, vegetables and other supplies would be picked up from the nearest town, but the butcher, who would display everything for us to choose, would truck the meat around. We had many friends staying at the same place and we all considered these weeks the perfect holiday. We looked healthy with our bleached hair and suntans.

Eventually we became more sophisticated and went out to dinner at restaurants like Fred Rigoni's, The Hungaria and the Rendezvous Cafe. Here we had our first European meals, Schnitzels with red cabbage for example, and drank sly grog out of coffee cups as there were no licenses to sell alcohol. If we wanted to party on, the taxi drivers would know sly grog sellers and we would pay through the nose for very bad liquor. We still had six o'clock closing in all hotels. For elegant eating with appropriate wines, we would go to *The South*, the grand hotel on North Terrace, with imposing Louie Cotton the Head Waiter in full control.

You may find this hard to believe, but the 1930s and 1940s were a joyous time to be living in Adelaide.

3

Carlien

Growing up meant more freedom at home, good parties and meeting new people. I found a soulmate at work called Carlien; a smashing looking girl, statuesque, fun, highly intelligent and like me, looking for more than a job at ETSA had to offer. So we planned the big holiday in Sydney. We thought we were pretty cool and Sydney was lucky to get us. Big mistake!

A chance meeting at a risque party at Waterfall Gully before we left, given by a real estate husband and wife team would affect my later life. The husband wore two sequined bimbos, his current lovers, on both arms – very bad taste! The evening dragged on in a most unpleasant manner and I would guess by the suggestive remarks, group therapy in the bedrooms was the name of the game.

I was planning to leave when I heard a frightfully English voice saying, 'Have you heard the one about Charlie who don't go for that crap?' I turned around to see an attractive guy with curious skin. He gave me the eye and then wandered over and introduced himself as Timothy. I found this witty, charming Englishman who lived in Sydney appealing, until he suggested I try him in bed. I replied haughtily that I was still a virgin and he appeared genuinely shocked and made some abstruse comment about there still being one left and asked what I was doing in a place like this. Most of us *were* virgins, no pill in those days, and of course God was checking us all out personally! Anyway Timmy went back to Sydney where he was a pilot with Qantas, but he left me feeling curiously disturbed or was it dissatisfied?

A delightful young man called Roy James came into my life. We fell very much in love, me 18 he 19, became proudly engaged, bought a block of land in Somerton, and planned our future home. I had the responsibility of the 'glory box' (dear God from whence did this name come?) where household linen and appliances, fluffy nightdresses and the one book on 'how to do it' were packed. Roy was incredibly sexy and my virginity was in constant jeopardy and of course was eventually exquisitely lost. Sweet first love!

Joan Limb (Bobby Lim's niece), John Walsh (Oriental Hotel), Roy and me

We bought a yacht that tipped over miles from shore. After swimming to safety in a pitch-black terrifying night, abandoning my yachting blazer and French sandals, and without making any attempt to save each other, we quickly and unanimously decided we were too young to marry. Returning the ring, (with oceans of tears) but believing we would return to each other, I took off with Carlien to Sydney.

With maturity I'm sure Roy and I would have had a great life together and I've always secretly hoped we would have another chance. What a delicious hunk he was!

Deciding to aim high, we booked into the Hotel Australia in Sydney for a week. Management introduced us to American Davis Cup players Dick Savitt and Art Larsen who were also guests. This was to be our initiation into the real world and we were running for cover in no time at all with the boys in hot pursuit. Instead I contacted safer friends from school days and they showed us Sydney. I cried all night for Roy but like millions before and after us, we fell in love with the place and decided to stay.

Due to a shortage of money we moved into a boarding house called Tudor Hall at Elizabeth Bay. This was a beautiful old building with high entrance gates adjoined to solid pillars and majestic marble steps leading to the magnificent entrance. Elaborate carving brought a touch of baroque to the stone urns placed in shady corners along the circular driveway. Roses drama-tised the balustrading and cascades of varied colourful flowers from a simple stone pot seemed to say 'Welcome Young Innocents'. Entering through the engraved-glass double doors was an elegant foyer leading to a splendid sitting room and then on to what, in the past, would have been an extravagant dining room. There were still faded chintzes and damasks and enormous gilt mirrors and dark oil paintings of rather pompous looking personages.

We just adored this place. It was full of an interesting mixture of young people. Sam, whose favourite expression was 'Holy Zamboli' was a warm, generous country lad, whose great passion in life was his racing-green Morgan. He also owned a disreputable motorbike on which he took Carlien to Newcastle (in shorts and bare back) and we carried her off burnt red raw with legs that remained bent for a week. I can remember getting stalked by a couple of sailors in Kings Cross and locking myself in a phone booth leaving them caterwauling on the footpath. I rang Sam for help and around he came with the boys from Tudor Hall to save me. They put on a great act, and the sailors departed hastily.

I remember amongst the many other boarders, an architect called Sally, a law student called James, Steve an ex-navy bloke, Patricia a musical comedy star with her baby, and Pamela, a pill-popping druggie who was engaged to someone 'in paint'. We never quite knew about Pam's elusive fiance but she was funny and had great clothes we could borrow.

We had a housekeeper called Mrs Douglas who cared for us and let us owe rent when we were broke. She was such a kind woman and we always honoured our commitments. It was a happy commune. Carl and I got jobs, ate at Kings Cross and adored the lifestyle. Everyone at Tudor Hall shared clothes, food, laughter and lots of secrets.

Carl and I were invited to the opening of the State Opera Company and had nothing to wear. So Carl dyed black a blue-and-white-striped cotton frock, bought a length of cheap red-and-white-spotted cotton and made a big sash, which she tied in an enormous bow on the hip. I bought some bottle-green-and-black Egyptian-motif cotton material for 7/5d, gathered a waist and joined it on to a bit of black material Mrs Douglas gave me. I cut out a round neck (no facing!), put on a wide black-patent belt and Clark shoes and pinned myself together. And of course, I wore my Grandmother's gold Spanish earrings I had never had the courage to wear before. We were photographed for a society paper: the caption called us 'Two elegantly dressed Adelaide girls'. We collapsed with laughter as Carlien had us imagining what could have happened had my safety pins come apart.

We were in trouble with Mrs Douglas. She called us to the bathroom where Carlien's black dye had taken over the pink marble bath. This Roman-style bathroom had the palest pink marble walls and floor with matching columns and dignified steps led up to the bath. It was exquisite and we were really upset at the damage we had caused. It took us weeks to get rid of the stains but we were so elated at our successful night that it was a labour of love. Mrs Douglas, as usual, forgave us.

We had a miserable Christmas however. We were stony broke. We'd sent telegrams to our parents for money but as they did not approve of our extended holiday they ignored our pleas. We'd made our bed, so to speak. So we dined on boiled liver and stewed, I mean *stewed* cabbage from a Chinese shop.

However we had fallen under the spell of Sydney. I worked at Nicholsons music store and Carlien worked at Palings music store with Jill Perryman. We were regulars at a nightclub called Regs, we had a room with a view of the Harbour (I still miss it), and stacks of eager escorts. I can still almost taste Cahills hot-caramel ice-cream cake and the Trocaderos scrambled eggs at the Cross they were so good! We all shared cabs to work as it was cheaper than public transport. It certainly didn't seem like work to us; it was just fun.

Carlien was a girl who lived and laughed every moment. She was generous to a fault and would help anyone with her last bob, but she never paid her bills and drank to excess. In Sydney she discovered sex and it became her favourite sport.

We were both only children and were competitive like sisters. She warned me that some of my new boyfriends were on her pending list. An elegant, and despite her excesses, extremely intelligent person with a riotous wit, she delighted in making me choke with laughter at the most inopportune times. Her father was an uneducated, competent tradesman from German stock, a heavy gambler and drinker who realised through his own lack, the importance of education. Being bereft of grammatical skills, he organised Sunday mornings as a Carlien learning time, reading newspapers and absorbing new vocabulary from the dictionary. Her mother was from an impoverished family, had poor diction and no education, but was amazingly artistic and made tasteful clothes for her only daughter. Carl was beautifully spoken and her hair tastefully coiffed in her unique style. Oh my, did she annoy some of my priggish Adelaide private-school counterparts!

I remember Tudor Hall as a happy place and I remember the kindness of dear Mrs Douglas. We swore if ever we made money, we would buy all those wonderful old homes and find Mrs Douglases to run them for homeless youths. One could not be unhappy in such a place. With a Mrs Douglas to make us ghastly corn-beef fritters when we were broke and starving, and stacks of good friends and laughter, this was probably one of the happiest and most carefree years of our lives.

4

Timmy

One Saturday we went to the Roosevelt Theatre at the Cross for an advertised 'hot show'; entertainment we did not have in Adelaide. I remember the tall actor Chips Rafferty came into the theatre after the film had started, escorting a pretty young thing. From behind us a larrikin voice called out: 'You bastard, where's your wife and kids?' The audience broke up, and the poor young girl, obviously inexperienced, rushed out of the theatre in tears.

At interval, with flushed cheeks and hot fanny, I nearly head-butted Tim the pilot. I thought I had made an impact at the Adelaide party but as he didn't remember me and thought I was a Qantas hosty I was fairly miffed. However he took my number and said he would be in touch.

His call didn't come for some weeks and that suited as I was still suffering real pain and confusion about dear Roy and didn't feel like having to deal with anything that could be potentially complicated. Tim eventually arrived at Tudor Hall with flowers and took me to Rose Bay to watch the flying boats in action. I can remember repeatedly moaning something that sounded like 'holy cow'. Obviously there was more to watching flying boats than my mother would have wanted. She hadn't known about *lust*!

My previous experiences with lovemaking had been passionate

and loving but obviously unskilled as Roy and I began to under-stand our sexuality. Here was Tim, the experienced, ex-married, 'older man'. He was a superb lover, and even now when I remember, my toes go vertical! He was sensual and adventurous. Sex was an art form to be explored and enjoyed. That we eventu-ally fell passionately in love was simply a bonus.

Tim was a fascinating man. He was one of the first successful plastic surgery cases in Britain during the war. He joined the RAF, flew many aircraft including Spitfires and Beauforts and was one of the British elite pilots. He was a night fighter, was shot down in flames and was mentioned in despatches. He survived this horrific crash and his badly burned body, particularly his face, underwent numerous surgical procedures over months by a magnificent team of medicos with a newly developed technique. The surgeons satis-factorily transferred skin from various parts of his body to his face and built on new eyelids, ears and a mouth. So that explained the unusual looks I had noticed on our first meeting. Because he was so young and healthy and did not drink or smoke, his recuperation was satisfactory and the bonus was he was still handsome although with a totally different face.

It was only after he had been suffering dreadful screaming nightmares for quite a while, that he explained briefly to me what had occurred – the actual crash, the flames, and the incessant pain from the burns and the surgery.

His childhood sweetheart Fay stayed at the hospital and at his side during those appalling early days. They married but they were too young to withstand all the shocks and despite their sweet love and loyalty to each other they sadly parted. Timmy returned to flying.

Fay met Bruce an Australian RAAF airforce photographer, and they eventually travelled Europe, camera in hand. His photo-graphs of concentration camps such as Auchwitz and Dachau were hailed worldwide as a brilliant exposé of German atrocities. When I eventually saw some of these, I threw up all over the lounge and had nightmares for a long time afterward.

Fay and Bruce settled in Sydney, and Tim eventually came to Australia hoping to fly again. This he succeeded in doing, firstly with Trans Australian Airways and then Qantas.

We all became firm friends. When Fay and Bruce decided to move on, Carl and I took over their basement bedsitter next to the fire station in Kings Cross. We looked up to the pavement through a grille and we thought it was wonderful. Tim shared a flat close by with a congenial bloke called John Howie.

We made interesting friends who we met through Tim and work. Everyone seemed to visit us in our little Bohemia – our strange wee flat with a cosmopolitan feel. Our visitors such as Eric Joliffe the Pix artist, Rod Taylor the actor, and Patrick Penny who owned Penny's Restaurant at Double Bay, would rattle on the pavement grille and we'd let them in. We welcomed Sammy Lee (from the notorious nightclub), the Boyd brothers, Jack Davies with his very naughty records, wild-eyed New Guinea patrol officers, pilots and navigators from the airlines of the world and many airforce personnel. I didn't ever do a body count of how many we could fit into our flat, but I'm sure poor Mr Meeby, our landlord, had a fair idea!

Tim had the most amazing collection of classic jazz records dating from 1929. He had picked them up prior to the war and in later years on his trips overseas. Singapore Radio and Kym Bonython our Adelaide jazz expert, enjoyed access to them. I was happy and I like to think it was a happy time for others, many of whom had seen horrific things during the war years.

The strains of *I thought I heard Buddy Bolden shout/ Open up dat winda, let that foullll air out* would echo up the stairway. One could only hope the other tenants enjoyed the great music of James P,

Waller, Hines, Tatum, Teagarden, Bunk Johnson, Sullivan, Walsh, Jelly Roll and Billie with Wilson's piano.

Unfortunately we had difficulties with some of the uninvited callers who were madly in love with Carlien. I can remember some poor bloke trying to crawl in through the kitchenette window with me swinging the broom at him telling him to go home. One of her most ardent admirers had a magnificent Bugatti and composed excruciating love songs (which he shared with us at any old time). I suggested she tell him to go elsewhere but she said 'Darling, how can I be that cruel when he says I can drive his Bugatti!'

Of the many visitors we had, a New Guinea Patrol Officer called David Anderson was particularly interesting. We knew nothing of New Guinea and he told us true and awesome stories of his adventures. Perhaps it was an omen of what was to come.

Dear Mr Meeby did have complaints about our noise but he liked us so much; we brightened up his day. We had a problem with the fighting between the lesbian couple upstairs, Candy and Holly. Candy fancied Carlien and Carl used to play on it and give her the eye. One day after Holly had viciously taken to Candy with a swinging iron, Carl said she would fix it. I heard bursts of laughter and we had no further trouble.

Life was blissful although I hated Tim being away. He was on the two-week English run flying the intercontinental Super Constellations (affectionately called Superconnies) and I fretted. Carl was having a ball but I couldn't join her. Tim was feeling insecure with all these gorgeous characters calling, but he had no cause to worry. I was deliriously in love. He didn't mind Garth Pointon calling, a navigator from BOAC who would call regularly with Elsie. Canadian Elsie was married to an Aussie Airforce pilot. A generous but lonely girl who just couldn't hold her bourbon well, Elsie excused herself several times during a party to go home and 'turn off the pork'. Off she'd toddle with some character who'd screw the pants off her and back she'd come without blinking an eyelid.

Carlien was on with a Rhodes Scholar at one stage; she always went for quality. After four days, she arrived back at the flat looking dishevelled and told me in shrieks of laughter that Mr Rhodes never paid his bills and they had climbed out of the fashionable and expensive Gleneagles Hotel window at three in the morning by hanging from sheets. I was shocked but it was impossible to get angry with Carlien.

Another time, she scrambled through the kitchen window wearing a Jane Engels suit with the bailiffs after her. Jane Engels was one of the first boutiques to let the clients pay as they wore, but Carl with the best of intentions, forgot about paying.

One night she rang me at some ungodly hour to tell me she was being taken off in a Black Maria and would be in the local gaol – would I try and get her out? This I dutifully did with a lot of help from our friends. She had alcoholically swung a fist at someone who happened to be a police officer – oops!

She was popular at Penny's Restaurant as she was excellent company. Patrick Penny had converted the old family home in Double Bay into a fine restaurant. It would present one of Pat's specialities as a main meal each night. Here Carl and that gorgeous sexy actor Rod Taylor really fell for each other. They had a pretty hot thing going for quite a while and then he really pissed Carl off by leaving her to go to America seeking fame and fortune.

Carlien then had a brief dabble with a lass called Dana. That really did shock me. I popped around on invitation to Dana's flat clutching a bottle of champers and found them in bed together. They both hooted with laughter at the look on my face and proceeded to roll around the bed, obviously for my benefit. I felt a bit ridiculous may I say. Carl eventually arrived back at our flat a trifle shamefaced I thought, explaining that it was only a diversion – she really still preferred men but believed one had to sample everything in life.

Tim decided that we should move in together in another area inviting Carl to join us and share the rent and the company. He liked the look of some new apartments at Bellevue Hill called Lilianfels. So that's what we did. It was great except we didn't like our new landlady and absurdly nicknamed her 'Did Lilian fels or was she pushed'. She wasn't too wrapped in us either after we nearly burnt the flat down, accidentally of course. It was a fun area and Bondi was nearby. After tentative dabbles with Irish pilot Brian McCardle and French Pierre Mann, Carl met a genuinely good bloke, a blind pianist from one of the nightclubs. They really cared for each other but unfortunately he died and Carl mourned for a very long time.

John Howie, Tim's old flatmate, and his partner Elaine who designed and made wedding gowns for Grace Bros, moved to one of the upstairs apartments. I started working for Elaine. I couldn't sew well but I could use the power machines and did have a bit of a flair for the appliqué work. The wage was excellent, I had transport to and from work, and I could have time off to be with Timmy.

Carl was still at Palings and she and Jill were given freebies for the different shows from opera and ballet to magic. At one of the concerts a Jewish gentleman called Justus introduced himself to me. He was a Dutch tenor, brought to Australia by the Government to tour and teach. He commented on the coincidence of living next door to us and I vaguely wondered how he knew. As it turned out he window watched with his binoculars at Tim and I making love. He obviously enjoyed it because he became obsessed and I had a difficult time fighting him off. Finally we came to an arrangement – if I would go to his studio and meet his friends and fellow musicians, he would behave himself. Sounded good to me – and I did meet some interesting people; Igor Melnitzky the concert pianist, Goossens the conductor, singers, talented orchestral members and sculptors.

I also had a bit of a problem with Justus when walking home alone through the park one night. Guess I looked for that one! When I later returned to Adelaide I heard from Igor that Justus had tried to kill himself and I felt very bad indeed. In due course Justus arrived in Adelaide (definitely not dead), proposed on his knees in a morning suit and Homburg hat, surrounded me with flowers and offered a life in America living with his cousin the film star Albert Dekker. My mother's face was a study. So was mine!

I did wonder if Igor had told little fibs to get my sympathy, perhaps at the instigation of Justus. Who would know!

Eventually tragedy struck. My father was critically ill and Mother needed me home. I could not face leaving Tim – God I adored him! Carlien was having a bad run. A tram had hit her, several bill collectors were pursuing their money, and a bisexual had fallen in love with her and threatened all sorts of dramatic things. So she decided a change could be good and Adelaide was safer. Selfishly this pleased me as I really was dreading the return home.

So in 1949 at the age of 20, I left our beloved Sydney. As Carlien and I circled Adelaide in a DC9 I can remember us recoiling at the lack of vegetation and waterways and the flatness of the landscape.

I can also remember my mother recoiling from this dyed-blonde bombshell with the widgie haircut and the skin-tight black suit, with eye makeup and toeless spike heels. She was so embarrassed at my appearance. It probably was pretty dreadful but *I* thought I was hot.

Seeing Dad was a shock – he certainly was dying. One of Dad's brokerage agents had visited him with Egyptian influenza and due to Dad's lack of resistance, he was just wasting away. The doctors were flying in medicine from America, which kept him alive and Mother poor.

Tim was supposedly fretting in Sydney, but one of those 'good friends' wrote that in reality he was knocking off a hostie called Barbara. I had met Barbara and had to admit she was a smash however the fact that Tim couldn't be faithful for five minutes absolutely broke my heart. Adding to my pain and disillusion-ment, he was making love to her in 'our bed', according to Justus, who really got into the act by writing me descriptive letters. So I sent Tim one of my very bad poems, told him I would like to pan fry his balls and broke our engagement.

Then I had another drama. Tim started flying over on super-numerary flights given to him by old flying mates and begged me to forgive him and marry him. He tossed in his job with Qantas. I was demoralized and disillusioned, my father was dying and I felt obligated to marry a faithless, unreliable, unemployed man. Forever the optimist I believed all would be well in the end.

A wedding day was decided with only two weeks to get every-thing organised as Dad was fading fast. We arranged to have him helped out of bed for the wedding to stand with me in the lounge room. It was a sad day but my father looked proud. Mum catered beautifully as usual for the guests but I recall feeling lost. My precious father was dying and I just couldn't accept it, and I was marrying a man I didn't trust.

We had a bit of a scare regarding Tim's divorce because he had changed his name by deed poll. Apparently he hadn't robbed a bank, he just didn't like his name. Fay it seems hadn't sent over any papers but he assured me everything would be okay.

Carlien had met a charming bloke called Frank and they had

married just prior to our wedding so we four honeymooned together in a shack at Port Willunga. God works in wonderful ways. Carlien had always worked on the 'luck' contraceptive system that had worked well until she met Frank. Dear Irish Frank was so hot that she used to have multiples when he kissed her and the first time she got in the cot, she promptly fell pregnant.

The next few months were a nightmare for me. Tim and I lived at my parent's home, waiting for Dad to die. Tim was unhappy not flying and couldn't take any other job while waiting for answers to his applications around the world. So I worked at Philips Hendon and made enough money to support us. Having done an aptitude test, it appeared I was the most suitable applicant to work for a temperamental Dutchman. I then spent many hours of work time ducking various TV accessories thrown at me. I had felt proud about winning the job – what a joke! It was interesting though that the aptitude test stated that I had a temperament that enabled me to cope with irrational behaviour and violence. It was possibly another omen for my future.

Tim and I often rented a room at the local Broadway Hotel and made love all weekend, away from mother's ear at our door, and yes, Tim still made me yelp with satisfaction. What a lover!

Eventually my darling father died. I loved him so very much and I was with him when he drew his last breath. It was my first meeting with death and looking back now I don't think I mourned as much then as later. Strangely I missed him more after I left South Australia.

Timmy finally joined an airline in New Guinea. He planned to reapply to Qantas once there, and then, after spending six months with Mother, I was to join him. I was still chilly about his affair with Barbara and very emotional about my dad but as Tim loved New Guinea flying and kept on telling me how much I was missed, I felt optimistic we could make our marriage work. The six months passed slowly. Mother went back to teaching and I packed up the cotton frocks, and with an appropriate hairdo (Mother had very quickly de-blonded me) I apprehensively left for New Guinea. Dressed in pale blue and pearls (Mother's idea of dressing safely), I arrived by DC4 at Lae airstrip.

In 1951, Lae had 662 white residents and they all seemed to be there at a party of welcome laid on at the strip. This strip had a runway (which doubled for a road) and two galvanised-iron sheds for hangars. It was a warm welcome by a diverse group of people. Rum and coke, scotch, gin and very little soda were poured for what seemed hours and Tim appeared to be ecstatic at my arrival. I was assured that everyone's apparent happiness had nothing to do with the booze but I felt overwhelmed, happy and somewhat drunk.

Eventually, the tipsy-tired newly weds started walking to the honeymoon cottage. Along the way we collected Lamberto, the grinning new *haus boi* who carried my bags. He talked incessantly in pidgin with Tim interpreting, telling me how good he was, how much work he intended doing, how honest he was. By this time Tim and I were weaving down the middle of an airstrip. I was sweating, not perspiring, and could hardly wait to have a shower. We reached a sentry post and a New Guinea *polis duty boi* with bayonet cocked, demanded the code word to get through. Of course we didn't know it. Then I enjoyed my first tropical rainstorm, which suddenly belted down.

After what seemed hours, and a long discourse at Air Traffic Control, we were allowed to pass. We continued down a muddy track and dripping wet we reached home, a long and narrow rusty galvanised-iron shed with arc-mesh walls, a green cement floor and a hole cut in the front for a door. On the left was another piece of iron forming an annexe where I was amazed to see a royal-blue throne with steps. This was the toilet, and Lamberto's pride and joy.

The ceiling of the *donga* was art deco. It appeared to consist of various coloured combinations of parachutes, padded up for some reason. Timmy did not tell me for some time that the padding was mother, father, and baby snake ... and all their relatives!

My first house in Lae, made of tin and arc mesh

It was one of the rare times when I couldn't speak. Tim had worked so hard to make it 'homey' and I really didn't want to upset him about his obvious penchant for green paint which had been given to him by generous friends. Lamberto proudly displayed the teapot and asked what I wanted, '*Misis wanem? Misis likim tea?*' Nodding weakly I adjourned to the blue throne, ever so briefly. As I slid the underwear down, two little green frogs decided to jump up and I jumped out, minus my underwear. Lamberto and

Tim went into peals of laughter and the ice was broken. I had to take laxatives the next week due to my lack of enthusiasm for the blue throne.

Subsequently, I was to learn that one did not entertain when the *peepea man* (person who emptied the toilet) had not called. Whiffy! Timmy explained that the *peepea man* was scheduled to call every Wednesday to empty the reeking can. As there were eight *dongas* in a row, we also knew when anybody passed wind. This was a frequent occurrence with Ron the pilot next door a whizz on spring onions, and Stu Mac using his schoolboy talents to outfart him.

Tim gave me a book of pidgin English to study, taught me how to fix the kerosene fridge and lamps when the electricity was turned off at ten at night, and gave me an affectionate goodnight kiss but no cuddle. He departed next morning for Honiara, leaving me to what I believed would be a fate worse than death.

In time I learnt to duck frogs, spiders, snakes and Ron next door who perved on me through the wire walls and who definitely went through physical changes when I peed.

Lamberto was a fountain of information. For example I had the pidgin book in my hand and I told Lamberto that I wanted to move the kerosene fridge from one side of the room to the other. With my attempt at pidgin I said, '*push push bokis bilong mi long hap*' accompanied by exagerated gesture. He broke into ecstatic squeals, rushed out to our *boi haus* in the back garden (and I think all the other *boi hauses* in the area) and brought back an entire army of *haus bois*, all of whom were waiting in anticipation. I thought to myself, Lamberto has been through this before; I am being set up. And I was right. So we went through it again with all of them hysterical, and me aware I was not handling things at all well! It turned out I was inviting Lamberto to an orgy in bed. Had I left out the '*bilong mi*' and said instead, '*bokis ais*' it would have been okay. But it gets worse.

Another day I was cleaning out the fridge. We had a platter of mixed cold sausage, one of which was black sausage. And can you believe it, I said, '*Oh misis laik dispela black sausage.*' It was a wonder I wasn't done for dinner. Naturally any person not entirely moronic would have sensed danger; Lamberto had an immediate erection of massive proportions and I left the room hastily. Actually Lamberto was always getting aroused. I don't think I realised initially that his accidental rubbing against me was really quite deliberate. I certainly noticed the constant wet spots on his lap and had to eventually reprimand him.

One morning I was on the throne relaxing at long last and taking my time. All of a sudden from underneath I heard, '*apinun misis.*' I jumped off, looked down and saw two twinkling black eyes peering up at me. It seemed we bonded at that moment because from then on an unfamiliar native boy waved to me in a friendly fashion all over Lae, in fact I suspect the beauty of my lily-white bottom was a talking point in many a native village.

After settling in I decided to get a job. I applied to Qantas, was accepted as secretary, and in my bright blue uniform walked around to the Qantas hangar to introduce myself to my new boss, the Chief Engineer. I had been told he was a non-smiling man (what an understatement), a brilliant engineer and very fair.

He grunted, 'Good morning. Sit down and look at your desk,' which was in the corner of his office. That's what I did for the next hour, looking at the pencils, sharpening them and looking at the blank shorthand book and the typewriter. And I waited and waited.

Finally he growled, 'Let's do a letter.'

As I waited with pencil poised, I looked out the window as

everything started to move and I thought, 'My God, I'm having a heart attack.'

My first pencil broke. Then a car without a driver started to move and my second pencil broke. I shrieked, jumped around the desk and grabbed my new boss. As I looked up yelping I thought I saw what could have almost been a smile. He explained it was a mild *guria* (earthquake) and told me to call him Kit.

I excused my shaking body and went to compose myself in the toilet. I was so nervous, my stomach was gurgling and I had diarrhoea. It was good to just sit and relax and after a while I got my act together and went to the door to find I was locked in. Yelling wildly and pulling at the handle, I finally got it open only to see there were bars across the opening. I'd been in a long time but hadn't heard the native workmen nailing wooden slats across the door so they could renovate.

As I peered through the slats squawking, no doubt looking like some wild animal in the zoo, my boss of three hours ambled through the gent's door opposite, buttoning up his fly. I will never forget his expression! He sort of gasped, then choked, then doubled over and people rushed over thinking he was having a seizure. It was my finest hour, a great moment in the history of Qantas. I was a legend; the girl who made Kit laugh. He and I were mates forever!

On returning to my desk with an attempt at composure, I spied a native woman with a baby on one breast and a piglet on the other. I looked serenely at Kit and he definitely smiled.

I enjoyed working for Qantas. There was camaraderie between the pilots and the engineers. Of course the pilots were chosen by God, but they were good pilots; they had to be in Papua New Guinea or they ended up wearing the wings instead of the plane.

The weather was unpredictable and the airstrips were rough

and often dangerous. Sometimes the pilots had to circle waiting for a cloud break, and if fuel was running low they hoped for an emergency landing nearby. Nadzap was an accessible alternative to Lae.

The mountainous terrain rose to over 14,000 feet with high ground close to bases at Lae and Madang. Port Moresby in Papua had monsoonal weather and Lae an average annual rainfall of 230 inches (584 cm). Considering that most of this fell between May and December, flying conditions during those months were not always ideal. Weather could change drastically over 15 to 30 minutes. A flight into the Southern Highlands in fine sunny weather could rapidly turn into a crisis requiring all the pilot's experience and knowledge of the area to find a gap in the mountains through which they could safely fly. Instrument flying in these conditions was not an option. Radio navigation aids were of an elementary type in the 1950s and the mountains blocked out the signals. Since all five provinces of the extensive Highland areas of New Guinea under administration control were supplied with cargo freighted in by DC3s (or lighter aircraft when only a small strip was available), it was apparent that development of the these more remote areas was completely dependent on air communication.

To hear pilots speak of some of their experiences was hair raising. One told of how he had left Madang on the coast for Goroka in the highlands, a 35-minute flight in optimum conditions. He flew through the Bena Gap and as usual was unable to contact Goroka Control because of the high ground between the airfield and his aircraft. As he turned towards Goroka and established radio communication, he was advised that the airfield would shortly be closed due to heavy rain. He turned to go back through the Bena Gap and found that it had also been obscured by cloud. He had no choice but to make a landing on a disused missionary strip with *kunai* grass two metres high. He landed safely. No DC3 was known to have landed there before and he was unable to fly out until the grass had been cleared by local natives.

Our lifeblood – that great plane the DC3, on Lae airstrip

A similar incident involving a single-engined aircraft was reported. The aircraft departed Lae for a southern airstrip, the route to which was via Lake Tryst in the mountains. The pilot entered the gap to the lake and headed down it to the exit gap obscured by cloud. He turned back to Lae and this exit had also now closed. He had no option but to make continuous steep turns beneath cloud and close to the water for about 30 minutes before a small break enabled him to fly out of the gap and back to Lae. I've seen competent pilots walk off the strip white faced and silent after some of these bad trips.

A Department of Civil Aviation senior officer made the telling observation that 'New Guinea is being developed courtesy of the Pratt and Whitney Company' which was a reference to the engines which powered the DC3s and some of the lighter aircraft. He could have added, 'and the pilots who fly these aircraft'.

I can't remember how many times we wives waited at the tarmac for news, or sighting of a plane. And often the captain would have to make repeated attempts to come in. As we all lived alongside the tarmac we shared the worry and it bonded us. People who normally would not have socialised formed firm friendships based on anxiety.

The pilots were regularly reviewed – we called it 'Circuits and Bumps'. They usually went on the waterwagon for a few days and were a bit subdued before the make or break day. Testing at night was even more nerve wracking. The wind currents, rugged mountains, poor terrain, bad communication, rough landing strips and demanding engineers all added to the pressure. But those pilots left New Guinea knowing what flying was all about and indebted to Kit and his band of efficient engineers.

I was still getting nasty little surprises. I came home from work one lunchtime to find a naked Lamberto on my lounge room floor looking at one of Tim's magazines and wanking happily. When I walked in he didn't miss a stroke and sporting an erect penis he said with pride, pointing to the magazine, '*Dispela namba wan meri*'. I don't believe I spoke, mesmerised by the gushing semen. Once again I thought I was going to faint but I managed to leave the room with some decorum. This never happened in Adelaide! I remember shakily giving him the afternoon off and avoiding his eyes for weeks.

Lamberto was also going through a stealing stage that was not unusual in New Guinea. If something took his eye he would place the fancied article under or behind something, then move it from place to place, room to room, until eventually it would disappear. Of course, if I found it, there would a look of innocent but happy surprise.

I will never forget the day Lamberto got an electric shock. He writhed all over the ground, rolling his eyes, drooling from the mouth. He prayed to the *big pela* in the sky and his behaviour was impeccable for ages.

We had come to know and love Shiela and her husband Ralph who was an excellent jazz pianist. Like us, they had a great sense of humour and we happily laughed away the hours. Their house was the old Red Cross base during and after the war; a rambling home with *pitpit* walls made from plaited reeds and wooden floors – very rare in those days. They were an artistic couple and the place was full of charming objet d'art from their homes around the world, mostly with a story attached.

Shiela and Ralph Albrecht and friends at Aero Club

On the road to Bulolo, Judith and Ian Brady and Jack Bax on Stan's truck

It was very hard for Ralph whose family were tea planters in what was then known as Ceylon. His family had lived a privileged lifestyle until Independence in the 1940s when they had to leave the country taking very little with them. Shiela, the daughter of a British army Colonel and an Irish mother, was educated in England, Egypt and Singapore and still is the best cook I have known in my life. They were cultured, charming people and truly adored each other.

We discovered an old Aero Club iron hangar on the other side of the airstrip perfect for music and dancing. We found an old piano, another couple of musos and with Ralph playing the ivories and Shiela singing with her lovely Irish voice, all of Lae turned up for party nights.

Out came the ballerina dresses and the white tuxes and how deliciously ridiculous we were, walking over the airstrip in evening clothes carrying our shoes. It was a hoot going through the sentry areas trying to remember the code words, especially when returning a trifle tipsy, and unable to see the black-skinned *polis bois* in their black uniforms. I was invariably prodded in the stomach with a bayonet which did not help my digestion!

I can remember one night; we all wanted to go to the toilet, so we looked for a suitable spot outside. I started offloading the underwear including the lace pantaloons and lifting all the petticoats of the ballerina frock – I think there were five and they almost stood to attention with Lamberto's starching. Anyway, as I was bending over and peeing, the girls started to giggle. From behind me I heard a shuffling noise and to my surprise, on turning, saw the whites of a *polis boi*'s eyes. As they were not allowed to speak on duty he'd had to endure looking at my well known rear end, whilst trying to avoid wet feet.

Judith and Alan Brady were also our firm friends. He was a top engineer and we were shortly to learn Qantas was training Alan for overseas postings. They subsequently lived all over the world. However at this stage, young Judith had the worst house in Lae. Houses were almost unprocurable and I will never forget this one; there were walking planks for floors and the walls were almost nonexistent. Everything was made of rusty galvanised iron. Every now and then she would lose one of her three children and we would crawl around the floor looking through the wide gaps until we would see or hear the lost one. One night she was locking the back door (whimsical!) when the door and wall landed on top of her. So from then on, with no door to protect her, her *haus boi* slept on the doorstep – what a good fellow he was. Judith was a gutsy female from an artistic family in Brisbane. She coped magnificently in challenging circumstances in New Guinea and this experience was put to good use when they transferred to Indonesia.

Tim received news from Fay querying the legality of their divorce; something to do with his change of name. You can imagine how well this went down with me! Then Tim had an exciting offer to rejoin Qantas, and a prestigious new home was offered to us on top of The Hill. I was pleased for him. I had always felt obligated to help him fly with Qantas again. Even though he behaved like an arsehole at times he was basically a darn nice human being. But somehow it was an anticlimax.

We moved to a pleasant house, bought a smart green English car to replace Jeremia the old jeep, purchased new curtains and furniture and joined the golf club.

We had started, finally, to build a bank account and as Tim worked for Qantas now I sadly left my job and joined the English shipping company, Burns Philp. We mixed with the socially ambitious families, had a *haus meri* and *boi* in embroidered *laplaps*, and entertained lavishly. Shiela was visiting her parents in England and I missed the fun we had all had together and Judith and Alan's overseas transfer was looming. We were becoming so respectable it was boring. I'd toddle down the hill to see dear lonely Ralph – it was like a tonic to us both. He'd walk through his lush tropical garden followed by proud mother dog Julia and puppies, mother cat and family, duck, hen, and goose. Just like the Pied Piper Ralph would chat to them all whilst cleaning his teeth as he walked and I swear they answered him. Or he would sing to them.

I think it was around this time that I started to acknowledge that I was unhappy. In fact, I don't think I worried at all that Tim and I might not have been legally married. We certainly were not on the same wavelength any more; I played golf, and he found other interests. We rarely made love; the passion was spent.

Eventually we faced the inevitable. We sat down with a bottle of Dewars and talked things through and sadly decided to end our partnership – neither of us had the will to make it work. I guess we still loved each other in a fashion but we decided to go separate ways.

We made an appointment to see Horrie, the Commissioner. I wish I had a picture of Horrie's face when I tried to explain that we wanted a divorce, if we were legally married, but we weren't actually sure we were. He dragged out a bottle of Scotch whilst attempting to sort the matter out, and he and I had the rest of the day off playing golf.

Eventually he arranged some papers for us to sign and in a few weeks we were free. Tim and I held each other and sobbed. We both knew our marriage should have worked. We'd had so much love for each other and known real happiness only to throw it carelessly away. Now all we felt was a mixture of sadness and relief.

For a time I wept to Bruch's first violin concerto, as I couldn't bear to play the old jazz. I remember swearing off men forever. However I must have changed my mind because I then recall lots of parties and some very interesting males.

Dear Timmy found a new girlfriend. Time does have a way of healing.

Part 2

5

Stasiu

In the late 1930s in the Polish town of Ryczow, lived a talented and wealthy family, well respected, though not socially accepted because they were 'trade'. They had many stores throughout the country areas, selling everything from sugar and flour to meat and farming equipment. These stores provided a lucrative income for the family as almost half of the population earnt their living from agriculture such as grains, potatoes, sugar beets, flax, pigs, cattle and horses. The family also owned extensive unspoilt forest and waterways that they leased to the aristocracy for shooting and fishing. The youngest son Stanislau Antoni (affectionately known as Stasiu) envied the wealthy Counts their beautiful horses and saddlery, and the fine riding gear they wore.

Stasiu's mother was an accomplished pianist. His sisters were violinists and the boys played competent cello. Music and the Catholic Church kept the family close. They were all educated at Catholic colleges and this elitist private school education set them apart from the locals.

Though Stasiu was not musically inclined he was a brilliant student and he drove the priests to distraction with his constant questioning. He would not accept the Catholic dogma blindly and the priests were constantly forced to try and explain contro-versial subjects. He also kept talking about the danger looming for Poland from Germany and Russia, an idea that priests, family and friends would or could not comprehend.

Because he was considered difficult and rebellious he was con-stantly punished. He told his family that the priests used a form of *cat-o-nine-tails* to whip recalcitrant boys. Another punishment was isolation in the boarding school with a diet of bread and water. The priests' word was law, and some were ignorant, cruel and/or homosexual, but as Stasiu was a powerful sixfooter they didn't use the whip on him often. He was an excellent soccer player (his soccer friend became Pope John Paul II) and he was Junior European Champion chess player. These attributes gave him some protection from the ire of the priests.

Stasiu told his mother that some of the priests sent the boarders out on weekends to 'Jew-bait'. They were told to pick fights, throw stones and damage Jewish homes and shop fronts. The boys were expected to accept without question that the Jews caused all the bad things that happened in Poland. His devoutly religious mother found this anti-Jewish behaviour hard to believe. The Polish life-style revolved around the Church and the priests. Stasiu debated how the Jews, eking out such a meagre livelihood from their small shops, could possibly be a problem, but the standard answer was that Jews were only loyal to Jews and not to any country. Poland had the highest percentage of Jews of any European country but they were tightly controlled by the government and had limited rights.

Stasiu suggested in class that the Catholic Church should take responsibility for much of the poverty of the Polish peasantry, because they kept the people ignorant. His parents were called to the school and Stas was threatened with expulsion. Despite these many dramas, he completed his high school education and was sent to Cracow where he was to study engineering at Cracow University. But then Germany invaded Poland.

A small slice of Polish modern history since World War I. In 1915, the Germans drove the Russians out of most of Poland. In 1920, Polish and Russian troops clashed and the Curzon Line was proposed as the boundary between Poland and Russia. The Treaty of Riga was signed in 1921, returning to Poland almost all its eastern frontier lost to Russia, Prussia and Austria in 1793. Poland also formed an alliance with France in 1921 and in 1932 signed a nonaggression pact with Germany. This ceased on 1 September 1939 when Germany invaded Poland and Great Britain and France declared war on Germany. Russia invaded Poland on 17 September 1939, and on 28 September, Russia and Germany signed an agreement dividing Poland between them.

And so commenced the systematic acts of genocide against the Polish nation. The German Nazis destroyed the archives of the universities and demolished the science, literary and history faculties. Two hundred professors and Fellows of the Jagiellenion University were arrested.

The Polish pre-war government was in total disorder and most fled to Romania. General Sikorski, Premier of the Polish government-in-exile based in London and commander-in-chief of the army, found great disunity and tension among the Polish emigres evacuated to Scotland. He suspected a conspiracy between Great Britain's military and the underground army in Poland.

The German Luftwaffe started the bombing of civilians, repeatedly using incendiary bombs. They killed the Polish people as they worked in the fields. They attacked villages destroying historical buildings and monuments so valued by the Polish people. They targetted schools, hospitals and apartment houses and bombarded the helpless and unprotected.

A question Stasiu asked of many people but which was never answered, is why the 110 French and English divisions facing 25 German divisions were completely inactive at this time.

The aristocratic Polish Counts courageously defended on horseback against the 2800 German tanks. The Polish army had few arms against the 65 German formations of about two million men, 10,000 guns and mortars and 2000 aeroplanes.

The Poles fought valiantly but were hopelessly outnumbered and the Soviet/German nonagression pact guaranteed Hitler a free hand against Poland. He gave the orders that all men, women and children of Polish descent or language were ultimately to be killed without mercy.

The evil Martin Borman instigated the German plan of biological destruction to eliminate the Jews and work the Poles literally to their death. The Nazis wanted to get full economic gain from the hard working Poles before they killed them. They believed that executions, starvation, forced labour and vicious biological experiments would in time successfully exterminate the Poles, Jews and other Slavs. Hitler classified physicians, priests, businessmen, landowners and writers as the elite of Poland and ordered Himmler to destroy them all. In time, because he believed 'seeds had to be liquidated before they began to sprout', secondary school pupils were also snatched and eliminated. Thousands of young people were sent to forced-labour camps. They were not allowed to speak Polish, their names were changed, false birth certificates were issued and the Germans inflicted dreadful psychological and medical tests on them.

A register divided the non-Jewish Poles into Classes. Class 1 named Poles who supported the Nazis before the war and Class 2 were people who still held German nationality. These people were considered to have the potential for Germanisation. Class 3 were those of Polish German mixed marriages and sent to work camps and Class 4 were Poles of German descent but were sent to concentration camps like Auschwitz to die because they had become 'too' Polish.

Although the Germans systematically plundered Ryczow, Stasiu's family was left alone because of a deal Stasiu's father made with the Germans. Stasiu saw his father kneeling before the German officers slobbering with fear and pleading for his life and was so disgusted he subsequently slapped his face and never again acknowledged him as his father. However this enabled Stasiu to be concealed while he established a black market and organised the Underground movement in his town.

Disease had become rife particularly tuberculosis and rickets. Public executions started and the Poles were handcuffed, blindfolded and their mouths sealed so they could not yell out patriotic slogans. Sometimes there would be mass executions and sometimes it was just an individual. This became the preferred method of elimination for three million Poles while over three million starved and tortured Jews were killed in gas chambers and furnaces.

Approximately one million Poles were deported to transit camps where the mortality rate was high. Hundreds of thousands of terrified young children suffered appallingly. Those considered unsuitable were killed by intracardiac injections of phenol – the others taken for Germanisation. Thousands of babies were literally torn from their mother's breasts. The plight of the Polish children haunted the nation. The wonderful Polish women would stand at railway stations in the hope of helping them. Sometimes they were able to buy the children to save their lives.

The Germans took over the Bank of Poland and undervalued the zloty. The privations suffered by the Poles were monstrous: a pitifully low food ration, no clothing and no shoes. But the black markets ensured many survived. The Polish women smugglers risked torture and death with food stuffed into oversized busts and sewn into their petticoats and blouses. The Germans killed, beat to death or gaoled the Poles for any reason: having sex with a German, owning a watch, smuggling bread.

The Germans took over private and state owned property; industrial and commercial businesses, the large coal reserves, lead and zinc mines and steel and textile mills. Heavy machinery, locomotives and farm equipment were manufactured in Poland and there was also rich salt-mining. All of this was of great value to the Nazis.

With growing unease the Germans were beginning to realise that although starved, terrified and homeless, the Polish people were not going to be broken easily and their patriotism had strengthened.

Stasiu's father organised with the Nazis for his youngest son to be sent to a farm owned by a dour German couple. This would guarantee fairer treatment than most of the poor unfortunate deportees. The food was nourishing and Stas had a warm bed in the stable and the stable animals for company but he was not allowed to go to church or the movies, use public transport, be given cigarettes or write letters home. He was allowed a washing bowl in the stable and although he sat at a separate table he was allowed to eat the same food while in the same room as the farmer and his family. His reputation as a worker grew and he was frequently loaned out to neighbouring farmers. Eventually of course the Germans realised he could be worth more working in one of their factories and they came for him.

Stasiu tried to escape but was caught and had his jaw bashed and broken by a gun barrel. He was taken by horse and cart to the station and transferred to another town where he was to work in an originally Polish owned munition factory.

Here living conditions were dreadful. The food was foul, mainly potato-peeling soup, and sometimes a dry piece of bread. A Jewish doctor managed to steal some garlic and onions, which he gave Stasiu. He removed the two broken back teeth and kept Stasiu's jaw clean. Stas always believed this saved his life because infections invariably led to death. The forced labour workers died like flies.

It was fortunate that Stasiu was transferred to work as a mechanic on diesel engines. He found this work satisfying and had a natural flair. In due course he was rewarded for his efficiency and was given a 'ticket' that set out his accomplishments and was to be useful in the years to come.

Stasiu was known for his physical strength and intelligence, his loyalty to his country and his deep hatred of the Germans. Polish Intelligence knew he would be of use to them if they could get him to England for Intelligence training.

Stasiu's friends Billy and Stefan told me that the Underground smuggled Stas to England. He had to undergo a gruelling check-in, and after being cleared by security he trained for his future as an Intelligence operator. He was then flown out of England and parachuted back into Poland.

His orders were to gather information from other agents such as enlisted men in German prisons and Polish officers in labour areas in Germany, about factories, industrial figures and communication lines. He was to assist in organising underground courts of justice run by the Polish people and eventually to plan and assist the sabotage that was to become so effective.

Stealing from the Germans became a way of life. Many Poles destroyed their own homes, properties and stock to prevent them from falling into German hands. The railway workers sabotaged trains by adding sugar and sand to the fuel. Other workers burnt down everything from factories to ammunition dumps. They went into bars to drop typhus bearing louse into the collars of the drinking Germans. They wrecked the grain the Germans used for stock.

There were four political Polish parties based either in England or the Polish Underground. The Polish Peasant Party was democratic and supported the English-based General Sikorski. Sikorski believed that relying on the British was a mistake and he decided to improve relations with the Kremlin. However Poland was a country divided with strong historical suspicions of the Soviets. There had been wars with the Russians throughout Polish history; they had always aspired to take over Poland and many thoughtful Poles, including Stasiu, correctly believed Russia now had a major plan to do just that.

There had been evidence to support this suspicion; the corpses of 3000 Polish officers were found in the forest of Katyn and 9000 Polish officers had been imprisoned in Soviet prisons.

Young Stasiu was actively training the Poles in the use of weapons and ammunition. They met in private homes and were instrumental in break-ins of official supply buildings of ammunition and foodstuffs. He also kept them informed of any Russian activities and plied them with facts about Russian strategies and weaknesses.

Stasiu had a code name and was known to be a clever operative dangerous to both Germans and Russians. Ukrainian collaborators and any others seen as servile to the Germans feared him. When caught, these people were tried Underground by the Polish People's Courts and eliminated without mercy.

Stasiu managed to make contact with some of the poor lost souls in the 2000 prison camps but there was very little anyone could do to help those in the three major extermination centres. He did get into Auschwitz using false work papers and confirmed that the intelligence reports England had received concerning the treatment and the suffering of the imprisoned Jews were understated. Even a tough operator like Stasiu was emotionally scarred for life by what he saw and he told me he could never forget or forgive the Germans.

He continued to get in and out of labour camps, lifting morale, organizing sabotage and fulfilling his primary aim; to help organise massive underground intelligence networks. He made contact with some of his relatives in Sweden and enlisted their aid. One unfortunately was caught and executed.

The Scouts and Guides were brilliant couriers and intelligence gatherers, the older ones distributing pamphlets and scribbling grafitti.

Stasiu provided transmitters and receivers wherever they could be used to advantage. The sewers were useful for courier runs. The Polish resistance movement was ranked highly and greatly respected by both the Germans and the British.

Incredibly, in June 1941 Germany attacked Russia and in late 1944, the Russian army invaded German-controlled Poland. By this time the majority of Poles were prepared for the infamy that occurred.

The Polish communists were beginning to show their hand in support of Russia and other Poles joined them although the dominant feeling continued to be strongly anti-communist. Many Jews who had fled from ghettos joined the communists. They had constituted 25 per cent of the Communist Party membership in 1938 and the Warsaw Jews were amongst the most dedicated communists. Unfortunately this added to previously fed propaganda and fueled anti-Semitism amongst many of the Poles, some of which remains to this day.

The resistance movement was well organised. Thanks to the air-shuttle system, newly trained intelligence officers were dropped into Poland. The Poles successfully duplicated the German Cipher machine *Enigma* and they reported German planning for the invasion of Russia.

The Germans moved their rocket program to Cracow and as

camouflage, placed wooden cows and dolls around the area with washing hanging in the make-believe cottage gardens. Polish Intelligence was aware of the deception and recorded the tests. The Poles actually stole a rocket with minimal damage, dismantled it and sent the parts to British Intelligence. Thanks to the Poles the British were able to bomb the German rocket testing area at Peenemunde.

Even though Polish universities had been closed a secret university was opened in Warsaw and had 2000 students, and a clandestine university for Cracow, Wilno and Lwow had 1000 students. Amazingly, medical studies were held in Warsaw. There were many young people with minimal medical training who satisfactorily carried out operations and amputations, often without adequate medicine, lighting and water. Technicians, plumbers, carpenters and bakers all gave their skills willingly to defeat the detested Germans. The Poles also perpetuated theatre, music and the press in the Underground. The Germans always greatly underestimated the extent of Polish intelligence, courage and determination.

Word was out that the Polish uprising against the Germans was to commence and the date was set for 1 August 1944. The Poles gathered in small groups out of Warsaw practising with what weapons were available.

Approximately 25,000 Polish army were secretly stationed and readied by 5 pm on the first and the battle for Warsaw commenced. Of these 25,000 only about 2500 were appropriately armed and they faced approximately 16,000 well-armed German troops. Nevertheless, the Poles seized most of Warsaw by the end of the day giving them a feeling of elation. They held the city for a short while and regained some public utilities such as the gas, electricity and waterworks. The Scouts and Guides ran a clever postal service during the uprising. They were no older than 15 and wore the red-and-white armbands of the soldiers with pride.

German chiefs were becoming uneasy about their ability to quell the uprising, however Hitler's new Chief of Staff advised that air bombardment of Warsaw would commence as soon as they knew which parts of the city were in German and Polish hands. The Governor General, Dr Hans Frank, now swore to totally destroy Warsaw, and so fighting started door to door amongst burning houses.

Stan in the Polish Army

Stasiu was fighting for his life in this battle for Warsaw. He blamed himself when his battalion was almost wiped out after eating poisoned tinned meat deliberately left by the Germans, but witnessing how successfully this plan worked, he sent word to an Intelligence group and the Poles used this system on the Germans whenever they could. Littered with countless dead bodies the streets resembled cemeteries. The Germans used Polish captives to clear the streets. Stasiu's friends Louis and Stefan were amongst these men. This was rat-infested work (as in turn, the rats became food as the dogs and horses had long been eaten).

The Poles started using the sewers and when the Germans discovered this, hand to hand combat ensued and many a battle weary soldier drowned in excrement. The Germans mined and gassed the sewers trying to stop their usage. Even though the Poles lost more men than the enemy, 91 German officers and 3770 non-commissioned officers and troops were killed.

The Germans commenced shooting patients and setting fire to the remaining hospitals. Atrocities continued until finally, Russia decided to make airdrops of food to the Warsaw Poles and then attacked the German-held suburb of Praga. However Russia had ignored the Poles repeated calls for help until the week before the Polish resistance fell and many Poles were killed unnecessarily.

On the 2 October 1944, surrender terms were negotiated. Stasiu felt strongly that England had failed Poland, particularly in refusing to permit reprisal bombing and that Russia's plan to install their own people as rulers of Poland had succeeded primarily because of this. He also realised that because of his well-known political views it would be unlikely he would survive post-war Poland, and this could in turn create an unstable atmosphere for his family. He had always been actively anti-communist so he and many other Intelligence officers were advised to make their way to England with the help of Bulgarian couriers.

The Warsaw uprising doomed the Poles in the capital to defeat and decimated the Polish Underground. This was just what Stalin needed to accomplish before his armies could occupy Warsaw in 1944 and become the rulers of Poland.

The Russians immediately placed people loyal to Russia in strategic community positions in public utilities such as public transport, gas, electricity and waterworks. And most importantly they were in control of the media. In disbelief and shock the Poles realised that this preplanning ensured the Russian control of Poland.

Stasiu never trusted the media again. He believed that whoever owned the media could control the country. In this case it was Russia who dictated what was acceptable and as we know they controlled many European countries for many years. Stas was aware of the likelihood of bias in reporting and he knew that given a chance, most governments would use the media for their own political gains.

Stasiu was a 22-year-old man in 1945; tough and fierce with a brilliant intellect; a law unto himself. He couldn't remember when he last slept in a bed, had a bath, sat on a toilet or cleaned his teeth. He didn't want to remember how many people he had killed, or in what way he had killed them but he knew he would never forget the horror.

He had eaten grass when he was starving and dog was his favourite food. The best meal he had eaten in years was a hot loaf of bread he had stolen from a German bakery. It was so delicious he decided to make it last for a day and he cried like a child when he realised he had gulped it down in a few seconds. He had never had sex and his mother's arms were the only ones that had held him close. He carefully made his way home to his family in Ryczow pilfering transport, fuel and food, crawling through sewers or hitchhiking when possible. He approached his family home carrying a stolen pig under his coat and cut its throat as he arrived. His mother and sisters cooked up a Polish feast with many of Stasui's favourite dishes, but he had starved for so long that he couldn't keep anything in his stomach.

Six million twenty-eight thousand Polish people died during the Russian and German occupation. Half were Polish Christians and half Jews; victims of prisons, death camps, raids, executions, imprisonment in ghettos, epidemics, beatings, starvation and excessive work. The Germans had taken many of the townspeople of Ryczow to unknown places. On Stasiu's return there were few neighbours and friends left.

Stasiu's family sadly agreed he should go to England and they would not correspond directly. Couriers would get news of him via other countries and hopefully letters would be sent through Swedish contacts. The titles of the family's leasehold properties remained intact and Stasiu knew his family would survive.

He packed a few pictures of them all, some food and a little money, and the long trek to England began. On arrival the British authorities installed him in a magnificent castle that had been converted for use by the Intelligence network. Here he was to undergo a gruelling debriefing in which his honesty and integrity as a Polish patriot was tested over and over. Warned to keep silent about his past actions and exhausted at the end of two weeks, he was allowed to leave.

Now he was on his own.

6

The ship

There was a strange atmosphere in the Cairo bar; a hum of excitement, sly looks and furtively huddling men. He sensed, almost too late, there was trouble looming.

He was making a play for a well-proportioned Arabic lady, his hand moving up her legs under the tables he seductively mumbled Polish obscenities. There could be no doubt about his intentions. She was squirming with pleasure. The sensual music and the heady smells of the Arabs, their pipes and spiced foods in the nightclub, intensified their passion.

His warning bell rang just in time; he turned to find the unpleasant sight of three knife-wielding Arabic men about to decapitate him. The handsome blond Polack threw his chair at them as he ran and the lady's ample bosoms landed in the lamb stew. He weaved through the narrow winding streets of Cairo with his inherent instinct for survival and sense of direction that had helped him during the war. Once again, it didn't let him down and he made it to the ship.

He worked in the boiler room of a filthy, rusty English merchant ship enroute to Australia. The crew was a motley unwashed mob; most of whom pulled their working clothes over their pyjamas, worked in them and only occasionally washed their face and hands.

They knew him as Stan and they presumed he knew only two English words, 'fuck' and 'cunt', which he used expressively and often. He would strip to his shorts, tie a strip of cotton material around his head and work as only a Polak can. Everyone was frightened of him, including the Captain, but no one doubted his capabilities, and all avoided incurring his wrath. No one knew anything about him – he worked, ate and slept and rarely talked.

One morning after working a full night shift, Stan washed and went to the mess hungry for breakfast and was served a piece of salted fish four inches long with dry bread. He picked up his plate, walked unannounced into the captain's quarters and threw the plate across the room, adding 'fucking cunt' in his guttural Polish. The captain had the good sense not to move or speak but arrangements were quickly made for bacon, eggs and potato cakes to be served.

It was not a happy ship, and there were bad feelings now between Stan, the crew and the captain. The crew deliberately tried to goad Stan by putting obstacles in his way and making his working conditions as difficult as possible and he infuriated them by ignoring them. The ship was unloading and loading cargo in Melbourne and Stan was determined to land there without mishap.

On landing he went ashore and found a Polish Club full of fellow Poles who greeted him as a brother and took him to their accommodation. Stan revelled in the warmth and caught up on Polish news. He also learnt that jobs were available for diesel mechanics in New Guinea so he jumped ship, bought himself some decent clothes and went with a new friend interpreting for an interview with the Commonwealth Department of Works. Stan was accepted for work in Rabaul, New Guinea.

7

Rabaul to Bulolo

After many hours of flying in a DC4, Stan landed at Rabaul airstrip on the Gazelle Peninsula. Walking over to a long shed that served as a terminus, he puzzled about the strong smell of sulphur.

In time he was to learn that the sulphur fumes were caused by a semicircle of volcanoes around Simpson Harbor with Matupit, the most active, frequently rumbling and spewing ash in the area. Light earthquake shocks called *gurias* precede actual eruptions. If the *gurias* built in intensity and frequency the town started planning evacuation. The sulphur smell was Stan's first awareness of something different. (As a sad point of interest, beautiful Rabaul no longer exists; it was destroyed when these volcanoes erupted in the 1990s.)

Stan walked around the town and felt optimistic for the first time since Warsaw. The sultry warmth of the place, the palm trees, the tropical flowers, the glorious coastline with its dramatic cluster of volcanic islands, were all fascinating to him. Also there were the dark-skinned girls who gave him questioning looks which excited him.

The harbour was magnificent, and he found the *bung*, the food stalls in the Rabaul market, awesome. They were loaded with wonderful fruits and vegetables, fish and colourful jewellery sold by happy, handsome native people. It fascinated him that Papua New Guineans were amongst the first farmers.

On his arrival at the Commonwealth Department of Works he was met by a fellow Pole who organised his orientation and then took him to some reasonably priced accommodation.

They wandered down to a local hotel for dinner with three Polish workmates; Alexander and Michael had been Russian prisoners in Siberia and Willy, who was on a full English pension. He had been in the Polish army fighting in the sewers when he was shot and left for dead amongst the other dead bodies. He lay for a long time with the hungry rats until someone discovered he was alive and dragged him to safety. Although medically unstable he had certain qualifications that enabled him to work and he was well looked after by the Poles.

Stan couldn't stop eating the beautiful tropical fruits and fish, and he started to enjoy living again. To speak his own language, to talk and compare appalling war experiences and discuss the Polish political situation was an emotional release.

The Poles found it ironic that the efficient swamp drainage and delightful buildings and boulevards in the township were the work of the Germans who administered until 1914 from the capital Rabaul what had previously been German New Guinea. It wasn't until after World War I that the League of Nations asked Australia to administer the area.

Stan's English gradually improved and Comworks was impressed with his work. No one was impressed however, when the boys took over the Comworks bar; they fought and yelled and abused each other. Then Stan would look around and growl, 'You 'ave drink with Stunly-boy' and the bar would empty.

The girls too had problems. They did not know how to handle the handsome Poles, Stan and Mick. Alex as it turned out pre-ferred boys, and Willy couldn't raise it, but the terrible twins were a nightmare. There were not many single women in Rabaul and it was against the law to take a native woman; Australia had an obligation to protect and develop New Guinea and they did it with integrity.

And then 'Stunly-boy' spotted the novice nuns and made his move. Many a novice decided against her chosen profession as Stan went through them like a dose of salts. Fortunately, the Mother Superior didn't catch him, but the word was out.

There had been 97,000 troops stationed at the Gazelle Peninsula during World War II. In his work Stan found rusty Japanese war-ships and planes. There were intact boats in caves at Tavui Beach. During Japanese occupation the Japanese headquarters had been built in a concreted cave beneath the town and he discovered legible military maps cut into the walls.

His work was varied and included upgrading the German built road networks which were laid out originally to connect their pro-ductive plantations, repair work after *gurias* and maintenance of the airstrip. The airstrip was spectacular because the Matupit volcano was in a direct line from the end of the runway and the aircraft had to turn sharply on approach. He found the history of the province of New Britain interesting, particularly that brief German involve-ment prior to the war.

Stan respected the Tolai people and the major ethnic group known as the Mataungan Association. These people were inde-pendently wealthy, growing coconuts and cocoa and opening successful trade stores in East New Britain. The Mataungan Association had the nickname 'Rabbal Rousers'. The members were militant and racist; a proud people against what they saw as white domination. Stan respected their passionate wish to be independent although he didn't become involved in the politics.

A strong 'cargo cult' had developed in the area. The local people believed that a new paradise would be heralded by the arrival of a supernatural cargo of goods brought by the spirits, the white foreigners, on the incoming ships. Variations of this strange cult appeared throughout the country. A Tolai leader announced that a shipment of free goods was arriving for the Tolai people and everyone stopped working to wait at the docks. Fortunately for the gardens they were tending, the administration demanded that the Tolai leader state the arrival date, and when he couldn't and no goods arrived, they returned to work.

Stan and his new friends bought a boat made by the Tolais and spent many happy hours in Blanche Bay, the flooded crater of a volcano that formed Rabaul's beautiful harbour. They fished and dived around coral and wrecks and as they had not known swimming as young people this was a great pleasure. Originally a volcano, The Beehives, in the centre of Simpson Harbour was a fascinating area for diving. Despite threatening eruptions they climbed volcanoes, such as Matupit, and hunted for war relics and Japanese tunnels.

As cynical as the Poles were, even they found the firewalkers from Baining Village incredible. Large bonfires were built and the adult villagers dressed in masks resembling animals and birds would dance through the fires, kicking the glowing red wood into the air. Wood was added and the young ones would follow.

These men from Poland were still haunted by the past, but they enjoyed themselves in this new country. Stan had received a letter via America from his sisters and even though things were bad in Poland, his family was living reasonably well.

Stan noticed his boss's wife had hot, inviting eyes and enormous breasts all pointing it seemed, in his direction. She also managed to be around his workplace and the Club and in due course when her husband was in Kavieng, she approached Stan, invited him home and an affair started that lasted many months. It was unashamedly sexual and of course in time Stan was caught, not only with his pants literally down, but also in the boss's bed. His boss was luridly descriptive about his intentions so Stan wisely fled Rabaul whilst still *intacto*. He hastily farewelled his new friends who planned to join him later when he decided where to settle.

When gold was discovered in the Morobe District in the mid 1920s, Lae village was chosen as a supply base to airfreight the gold dredges via modified Junker aircraft to the Bulolo mines. When the gold was depleted Bulolo Gold Dredging, an American company based in Morobe Province, decided to transfer to timber which it believed could give New Guinea future economic independence. Eventually one of the largest plywood factories in the world evolved in Bulolo and lumber, reforestation, a School of Forestry and experimental tree farms were all part of the plan.

Bulolo Gold Dredging was taking on workers and Stan was employed driving the huge diesel logging trucks down a 'heart-in-the-mouth' road to Lae.

Life was agreeable. The Company provided him with a pleasant, furnished home and the Kellys, a generous Australian/Irish family, befriended him. The Americans paid well and he gained new skills and confidence. The employees bought all their supplies ranging from meat to rum at discount through the Company store. As in all logging camps the men worked and played hard.

On one visit to Lae, Stan nearly killed himself on the old Bulolo Road. This led him to realise the hazardous nature of the roads through the mountains, something that was to prove useful later. That trip was also memorable because he chatted up a girl of mixed race named Dot who was working in the Hotel Cecil. She was a pretty girl known for her enormous breasts and minute brain. She and Stan hit the hotel and the whisky in Lae, and in no time at all she was in his bed and purring. He decided to take her back to Bulolo with him. Everything was fine for two years but eventually she grew bored with the inactivity and the smallness of the community and left for Hong Kong with another man. The story I heard was that 'they were chased out of town by an irate Pole in a fast jeep toting a fast gun.'

Stan sulked for a while and when recovered seduced a married woman called Roma who fell desperately in love with him. It became torrid indeed and once again Stunly-boy thought it wise to move. Especially since Roma was pregnant! She had a beautiful son with blond hair and very blue eyes.

Stan moved to Lae. He went to the Hotel Cecil and met Ma Stuart, the owner. Everyone knew Ma had looked after Errol Flynn for years; I'm not saying Stan conned her but from the moment of meeting, Stan was assured of 'Errol's annexe' at no cost except an agreement he would pull his weight around the hotel.

Stan's presence did not go unnoticed; he looked great, the women adored him and the blokes didn't argue with him. He was loyal and considerate to Ma and contributed greatly in the running of the hotel. They were genuinly fond of each other and retained a firm friendship over the years (unlike Errol Flynn who owed her thousands but snubbed her when she visited America).

The story goes that Ma who was a strong Anglican, attempted to feed and clothe the alcoholic Anglican priest in Lae. He relied on his flock for monetary donations that provided him with the numerous bottles of Scotch he consumed, but he was starving to death. Ma decided that Polish Catholic Stan would visit each day with food. Stan was too much for the priest, who gained weight, wrote passionate sermons and never drank again. Ma referred to it as another of God's miracles. Stan who saw it differently said, 'The poor bustard shit-scared I kill im.'

Ma asked Stan not to drink in the bar until late at night. He gave her a quizzical look and asked why and she replied that she wanted to keep her clients. Late at night in the Hotel Cecil could be heard a deep growling 'You have rumbo with Stunly boy?' Sometimes Stan misunderstood his unfortunate drinking partner who would wonder why a madman yelling in a foreign language grabbed him around the throat.

One night in 1952 he was carelessly slumped over the cocktail bar talking to a carpenter called Harry, a loudmouth drunken gambler, when he noticed a girl with long blonde hair, enormous brown eyes and glowing skin dressed in voluminous grey chiffon. He mumbled, 'You get broad's name' and Harry, like most people, obeyed. Lae's population had soared during the fifties with an influx of interesting women. But Stan liked this one. He lurched to his feet and stood against the door, willing her to look at him. He became frustrated at her apparent lack of interest and what appeared to be arrogant scorn. The more she ignored him, the keener he became. However he was a shrewd operator. He growled to Harry, 'Stunly boy play good game here – I fuck this broad, you see!'

8

Lae

I was gradually picking up my life again after Tim and I had parted. Divorce does take its toll. In our case, after the initial feelings of relief came the sadness of a love lost, loneliness and the questioning. I knew it was time to move on, but I wasn't sure how. I kept remembering Tim, his sweetness *and* infidelity, and I came to realise that had I been more grown-up we could probably have worked things out. I was only 21. As an only child, I had feelings of guilt about leaving Mother alone in Adelaide after the death of my father, another factor undermining the marriage and contributing to its failure.

Tim and I found excuses to see each other, both of us unable to completely let go. Eventually we got our act together. Tim had to go south for training on intercontinental superconnies, and my life became deliciously decadent. I was courted, chased, spoilt and adored. I had fresh steak and oranges brought up from Sydney, records procured from America, perfume from France, and my new but empty house started filling up with friends and possessions from all over the world.

Food in Lae was still limited. We relied on the ship bringing frozen meat and vegetables. This was fine for three weeks but the quality declined for the next three and during the week before the ship's return the food was inedible. So I gave elegant dinner parties for a couple of weeks, and then enjoyed the dining and wining out for the next four, sometimes at the Hotel Cecil or the Lae Club but mainly at Qantas where the food was always reliable.

As emigres we were encouraged to employ indigenous people in our homes. We stressed cleanliness and hygiene, provided them with basic accommodation including their own shower and kitchen, and a ration; sugar, rice, tins of mackerel fish and bully beef, tea, biscuits and of course tobacco. And they were paid a small wage.

I could go to work each day at Burns Philp, (where everything was discounted for employees) and leave everything else to my new *haus boi/meri* team. What a wonderful existence; no washing, ironing or dishes.

I had asked Lamberto to leave because I did not feel I could, nor should, cope with his wanking habits. They had increased to mammoth proportions. He really did have a problem! As revenge for losing his position, he took my beautiful cat Bina and ate her in a stew and then told me about it. I had nightmares for weeks and to this day I still mourn for that darling deaf white cat.

Neeka the *haus meri* was a dear girl who cultivated a productive garden of native herbs. She loved my 'goings on' and her eyes would twinkle when I was dressing for yet another date. Once her shyness had disappeared, she was delightfully cheeky and would say, '*Im namba wan. Im push-push gutpela?*' I organised with Geoff, a pilot, to take her for a short flight from Ples Balus airstrip. She arrived home with eyes ecstatically rolling upwards to God in the heavens saying, '*Mi lukim balus* (plane) *and tok long big pela.*'

When I first arrived in Lae, a strikingly handsome man had affected me strangely. I often saw him about the place, even at the golfcourse, and when I asked around I was told he was from Poland and a bad bastard with the women. Then of course,

I remembered Shiela's comments at the art exhibition so many years before. My eyes started to follow him, as did every other woman's it seemed, and I was peeved that at social occasions he seemed to ignore me. He was a superb and sexy dancer, but he never asked me to dance and I longed for him to look into my eyes and flirt as he did with others. One night he started to walk over and my heart pounded with excitement. I was preparing my answer when he walked straight past me and asked my friend Margie to dance. I was furious and sulked for the rest of the evening. Margie came back in a state of lustful hysteria and I sat miserably listening to her ravings about him. I didn't see him look at me once that evening, but I swore I'd get my own back for being ignored.

One night at the Lae Club he just stood against a doorway and stared at me for what seemed hours. It was too much for me. Pretending to visit a friend at another table, I put on my best private-school voice and said haughtily, 'It's rude to stare' as I looked up into his gorgeous, mocking blue eyes.

He replied, 'You wrong – I look, you stare!'

I shook with rage.

One morning Shiela who had arrived back from Europe, rang to say Bulolo Gold Dredging had employed a man called 'Horse' from somewhere in Europe, to dive in the thick black mud and bring up the dredge buckets which had been lost in an accident. Everyone was going down to watch as rumour had it this man was so strong he could probably lift them out without assistance and that he had once lifted a Volkswagon car with one arm! So down we went and I nearly fainted. There he was, my fantasy man; a divine semi-nude body diving around in the mud being cheered by everyone each time he brought a bucket up. We were drinking champagne and he was offered a glass before he dived – I thought he lifted it and toasted me, but I couldn't be sure.

Everyone drank all the time in New Guinea – we needed little excuse. So we partied on until it started to get dark and was time to go home. As I turned, something wet and slimy touched me and I looked into mischievous eyes.

A guttural voice said, 'I'm sorry – I leave mud on your pretty frock – did you enjoy me today?' I mumbled something totally incoherent and stumbled on my way, trembling from head to foot.

One morning my boss informed us we had to move office to another area as there were renovations to be done and guess who was the renovator! Every day I suffered watching his flexing muscles. I was obsessed. I'd ring Sheila at her office and give her a stroke by stroke description of his movements, and briefly I'd feel better. I might add Sheila adored Ralph her husband but attractive men were to be savoured.

The New Guinea *bois* revered him and it was fascinating to watch their response to his orders. The more he roared at them the more they loved him and the harder they would work to please him. And he always acknowledged a job well done. They would squirm with pleasure. (I would have too, given the chance).

Things went from bad to worse. I was so obsessed with this man that I couldn't enjoy myself with other friends. Geoff, my Qantas friend and frequent companion, was annoyed and said he felt superfluous.

Ma decided to throw a fundraiser for the church. Other organisations saved the local newspapers and sold them to the natives who rolled their tobacco in a sheet and made cigarettes, or raised money by holding practise baptisms; a shilling for a dunk in the river. But Ma gave value for money. She arranged a boxing match to be held at the side of the hotel, having conned the potential 'prize fighters' from all over the place. One was the manager of Steamships Store, another the local Catholic priest. There were a few strong no-hopers, including a couple of drunks and a local medico. They were promised no one would beat them up – it was all for show. She had the church committee roster the fighters; the biggest blokes would fight the smallest.

People came from everywhere; natives from the villages, plantation owners and Laeites all paid good money. We were a generous lot! The men wore whites (the equivalent of suits and ties) and we wore our ballerinas with layers of starched petticoats underneath a billowing frock, and we sat around the boxing ring; the seats of course were more expensive than just standing. The locals weren't charged entrance fees. The *meris* wore bright floral 'mother hubbards', cotton frocks gathered fully around the neck, and many of the *bois* wore Haiwian shirts.

We were handed glasses of champagne on arrival, topped up by hired waiters who walked around during the night with jugs of champagne and beer. Colourful tents were erected to house the 'prize fighters', and holes dug for the toilets. The mozzie machine, a truck that sprayed insect repellant, had been around earlier so we weren't eaten alive. In due course the fighters arrived, the Pole rather tipsy in skin-hugging red shorts, and the crowd went beserk obviously expecting something interesting. They weren't disappointed. He was to fight a scraggy little fellow with a wooden leg. We women howled with laughter! It was a good show. The little fellow won the fight of course, the climax coming when he eventually took off his wooden leg and pretended he was going to thrash the Polack. The Polack ran for his life.

Sometime later I meandered through the mob to the toilet. Suddenly I was grabbed from behind, swung around and kissed so passionately I was almost not breathing. I was red hot and shaking like a leaf. Then he left me without a word. I don't know how long I stood there and I don't know where I went but I did know that nothing would be the same. Ridiculous it might sound but I knew from that moment that I was at his mercy and I could not escape.

Weeks went by and I heard nothing. I felt drained with emotion. I had a half-hearted affair with a fellow workmate called Paul that smartened me up, not because he was the greatest lover, but because he stole the company's funds from the safe and tried to use me as an alibi. This was the last straw and I swore off men for life and spent all my spare time playing golf. I did see the Polack at a dance but was ignored by him. However it was satisfying to watch his face later when Paul and I danced; we always put on a sexy show and it did not go unnoticed.

One evening, weeks later, I was hanging curtains in my bedroom (I always seemed to be hanging curtains!) when I heard guitars playing outside. I went to the front window and could scarcely believe my eyes. Three native *bois* were strumming their guitars and one of Tommy Seeto's Chinese cooks was setting a picnic on the lawn, and there was the Pole, popping a cork from one of the champagne bottles. There were ice buckets filled with bottles of French burgundy and champagne, pretty crockery, goblets and napkins. Flaming bamboo torches lit up the garden and a great bowl of hibiscus flowers threaded on long fronds hung gracefully from a pedestal. My tongue was once again in a state of paralysis.

He said, 'You and me party – what you think?'

I think I nodded and stumbled to the rug. I do remember he handfed me with delicious crumbed prawns, pieces of Peking duck and Chinese pork fillet. I drank French champagne and burgundy and he kissed me so gently I thought I was going to faint. He was full of love, mumbling Polish phrases that I didn't understand, whispering something about giving me a child. I fervently prayed he would start. I think my sanity left for some time. Around 11.30 pm he asked everyone to leave, took me in his arms, said what sounded like, 'You lully darling,' and left!

Weeks went by and he didn't ring, call or write. Then finally about two months later he called into my office bare chested, wearing the red shorts and a matching bandeau.

He stated, 'My name Stanislau Antoni Rybarz, good Polish name. You love me, you call me Stach or Stasiu but with people, Stan. I pick you up Saturday morning. You pack up.'

And that's what I did.

9

Milford Haven

In a daze I climbed into a huge diesel truck with my possessions loaded on the back. We didn't speak at all as we travelled down the Milford Haven Road leading to the wharf and turned right into a rough jungle track. After what seemed hours of oppressive heat and silence we arrived at my new home. It was a small wooden shack perched on the edge of a creek; an almost empty wooden shack. There was no water, no electricity, no sink, no shower, but there was a big wood stove and a bed. And I didn't care. I was in love! Everything was left in the truck and we made love for the first time. It was wonderful but then I'd been waiting so long I was hardly a reliable judge. Amazingly I felt secure and contented without knowing this man at all.

After a while he said he had to go to work, and out of nowhere popped an old black man called Narku who was to be in charge of the house (and me). Narku was all smiles and Stach made several rude gestures and suggestive comments about what we had been doing and to my embarrassment Narku giggled and squirmed with pleasure.

I fancied a shower but of course I couldn't have one. My darling told me to dunk in the creek. I obeyed, feeling romantic. That delicious feeling disappeared when I heard boyish tittering and saw

Milford Haven Road leading to my third home,
a shack perched on the bank of a river

several little brown eyes peering through the trees. I made a run for it and once clothed and having regained some composure, I stood outside calmly waving farewell like 'the little woman' is supposed to do.

Under Narku's disapproving eyes, I unpacked and arranged my two rattan chairs, coffee table, divan and mattress and some greenery in attractive tubs. I realised that because of the holes in the walls the wind would probably dislodge ornaments so I only displayed a few. And of course I put up curtains! Again! I can still see the incredulous look on Stasiu's face when he walked into our little love nest.

Narku walked through the house with a look of haughty disapproval and seeing my good saucepans sitting next to his one old frypan and saucepan he went off in a huff. I was taking up too much of his space and I realised Stan was special to him and that I would have to be more considerate. Stan organised a bucket shower in one of the partitioned areas and we had to remove floorboards so the water could drain away. At first I found it daunting filling the buckets with creek water, but in time Narku and I formed a workable system whereby we always had hot water on the wood stove. The shower was okay as long as I remembered there was a hole where I stood; I think I often looked more like a deformed duck than a sensual nymph. And of course it took concentration and coordination to synchronise the limited water, bucket and soap when hair washing.

I decided to wash my own clothes after watching Narku swishing the clothes against rocks in the creek. I filled one of my large bowls with water boiled on the stove and washed each article separately. Hours were spent washing clothes, trying to keep my body clean, and learning to cook the Polish way.

Stan's English was not fluent but he was vividly expressive using his hands, body and intonation. He talked of his family and Europe, of politics, history and Australia. He was critical of the Australian education system and our loyalty to Britain. He believed we allowed our kids far too much freedom, too little culture and not enough discipline, that we were uncaring of our old people and that the young did not show respect, particularly of the elderly.

He explained the difficulties of being unable to speak a language and how he relied on studying people's faces to assist comprehension. He pointed certain things out to me which helped me judge character. This skill has rarely let me down. He also got out the chessboard and drummed strategies into my poor brain but at this I was a poor student.

Stan shocked me but fascinated me. He had a brilliant mind and I became addicted to his way of thinking. I had never known discussion like this. He was critical of my education. He asked me once why I hadn't studied world history at school. He said it appeared I knew only English history and I was an ignorant person. That went down well! So he taught me about the world. He firmly believed that Australia was the best country in the world but thought we would have to grow up quickly to compete with Asia. Unfortunately his views on our Unions didn't go down well with every one. He believed their usefulness was over and their power had to be broken if Australia was to have the ability to compete worldwide. Politically he was dynamite, unlike most Australians who were apathetic about politics in those days. He had no respect for 'lefties' (anyone obsessed with social justice) but believed in private enterprise and restricted government power, otherwise too much was given and incentive was lost.

By now, my absence had been noticed in the town. I had taken holidays but Tim found out where I was and hotfooted it to our little love nest. It was clear he was both worried and appalled. I in turn, made noises about his new girlfriend Jean. Stan was decidedly Polish about Tim calling and the atmosphere was chilly. Sheila and Ralph thought I was demented while Judith and Alan took it in their stride. I think everyone was curious how this amazing relationship would work.

Stan won a contract that was to take him away for quite a while. Of course I hadn't thought such possibilities through. When in love one is inclined to say things like: 'I would follow you to the ends of the earth,' not necessarily expecting this to be taken literally. After all I had just put up the curtains!

We spent the next couple of weeks making love, and discussing how I would survive without him. He tried to teach me how to use the strange iron that was heated on the wood stove but I changed it for a less challenging kerosene model. He taught me how to easy pump the lights and all I needed to know to cope on my own in this house with a few thousand unknown native people as my neighbours. He thought I should have a dog and I knew Julia, Sheila's English Setter, had just had a litter so I arranged to have one. They were beautiful, intelligent dogs and I decided on a little girl and called her Rebecca – 'Bekky'. I returned to work at Burns Philp and I saw Sheila and Judith when I could. I was overwhelmed with passion and I knew but didn't care that everyone was gossiping in the town. Stan was away for several months.

After what seemed an endless time, Stan returned and informed me, 'Mary friend of Harold come to live here and shooting practice start.' Australian Mary had been in the airforce and said she could shoot but I had never held a gun. She was tall, lanky and flat chested and seemed desperate for a husband. I scarcely knew Mary and certainly didn't fancy sharing a house with her and probably Harold most of the time and she was certainly not overjoyed. However Stan was adamant and Harry did as he was told. I guess Stan thought on the incompetence scale of one to ten, I would rate a one.

Bekky was brought home and after the dear puppy had settled in, Stan made plans for target practice. Bekky was tied to a tree away from the target area because Stan insisted she had to get used to the sound of guns. I did not think to ask why! And the shooting commenced. Because I had a good eye I did well with the 22 rifle. Mary ended up in jealous tears, the local natives were impressed and Stan patted me on the head and beamed proudly. Then I disgraced myself. I dropped a loaded revolver and everyone ducked. I was mortified but Mary couldn't stop smiling, suddenly she felt better. The puppy had a nervous breakdown and we all ended up wiser.

Narku, Bekky and I would wander through the jungle picking wild beans, ginger and a variagated leaf we called the *three-in-one*, a herb for cooking. When the ship *Bulolo* was late with the freezer food we ate tinned mackerel and that herb made it almost cordon bleu! One day after we had picked beans for our meal we stumbled on a long narrow *donga* about 50 feet long with arc mesh walls (similar to my first house). It was covered with vines and lichens but we pushed our way through and found an incredible arsenal of weapons; machine guns, rifles, grenades, all of which appeared to be in excellent condition. I wasn't sure what to do, but reported it to the police. It turned out to be a Japanese arsenal worth a great deal of money. I've often wondered who collected on it. It certainly wasn't me!

When Stan returned, Narku and I showed him our find and I was roared at for wandering around the bush behaving like a 'stupid broad'. I retorted that I had plenty of ammo with which to protect myself. That didn't rate a smile but I think he was quite pleased with me. He found it interesting that Narku and I were gradually developing an understanding of each other's cultures. Certainly Narku protected me well, but only because of his respect for Stan.

Native men 'ruled the roost' and generally women were not respected, in fact they carried all the heavy stuff, always walking a few paces behind their *pela*. It riled me that the *pelas* could have ten wives if they so wished, the women would do all the work and the blokes would get the profits.

I learned how to cook the native way, and as the ship *Bulolo* was often late, Narku taught me how to pick a freshly caught fish at the native *bung* and how to cook *kaukau* (sweet potato). Sugar cane, maize, bananas, cassava, yams and sago were our standard food.

Narku also taught me a great deal about the Morobe Province and Lae, the second largest city in New Guinea. I was amazed that a swimming area in the Butibum River used regularly by whites marked the site of the last raid on Lae by hostile tribes that killed 67 people. Before the gold rush of the 1920s and 1930s, Lae (originally spelt Lehe) was a mission station and when Rabaul erupted in 1937, Lae became the capital.

During the Second World War the Japanese used many parts of Lae as landing points. Australian troops landed on beaches and parachuted onto the Nadzab airstrip just out of Lae and after six months fighting during which Lae, Wau, Bulolo and Salamaua were all destroyed, they had the Japanese retreating, first to Salamaua and finally Wewak. In the fifties Nadzab was still in fair condition and used for emergency landings.

Narku was proud when Stan won the contract for the reconstruction of the old Wau/Bulolo/Lae Road and the Markham Road and various Bailey bridges over the Markham, Watut and Bulolo Rivers which were frequently washed away. This enabled major developments to commence, such as coffee and tea plantations, with Lae the major port.

I was beginning to understand how much Stan expected me to change and how enormously different our lives had been. I met quite a few homosexuals. I suppose I had met many in the past without knowing. There were numerous homosexuals working in New Guinea; the restrictions of southern living did not apply here and everybody got on well. A range of people from Europe and Asia started visiting us. I sidled around a bloke called Ray Spragg and his exquisite Chinese mistresses, hoping he wouldn't notice me (but he did judging by the look in his eyes). He was an articulate and impeccably dressed Englishman. I have no idea what he did for a living but he was obviously very wealthy. Rumour had it he owned brothels and ran drugs and he was supposed to be a remittance man. I thought him suave and I suspect there was no truth in any of the rumours.

I became skilled with the rifle and Stan had trained Bekky well. She would smell someone outside the house and follow the scent around the inside at the base of the wooden walls. When it reached the front wall she'd stop and point her nose upwards. I'd fire through the wire at the top of the front door, open the door and let Bekky out. There would be excitement, legs rushing through the undergrowth, and invariably the panicking would-be intruder would make for a tree. As he started to scuttle upwards Bekky, whose timing was perfect, would grab his *laplap* and patiently sit at the base of the tree, making ferocious dog noises, grinding her teeth, and playing 'bally' with the *laplap*. The terrified *boi* would perch up there until Narku arrived to check him out. By the time Narku had finished describing what Stan and the dog intended to do to the *boi*, my worries were over and Narku would let him go. Bekky won a biscuit and Narku a *laplap* and more importantly, respect from Stan. The door however was not a pretty sight!

Poor Mary was a cotcase. She was deaf in one ear and if she slept on her hearing side I had a good night's sleep but if she could hear anything well, no one slept! A small kerosene lamp was left on in her room all night.

Then she started to stutter. Life's not supposed to be easy, but I could do without a terrified deaf stutterer! As expected Harold stayed over more frequently, which annoyed Stan when he was back because we all sat up listening to Voice of America on the wireless at midnight drinking his Scotch.

Stan flew in for a weekend and I was chirping like a bird until he said, 'You get ready for big party. Cook for 15 *ciekawy* (interesting) people lunch Sunday – make plunty good *kaikai*.' I mentioned the two chairs and one small table and then I rang dear Sheila for help and as usual she rallied. I gratefully accepted her suggestions, borrowing furniture from Comworks using Stan's diesel truck (that I drove for the first time!) and as I heard the

Bulolo had shipped in some great steaks, decided on carpetbag fillets. I preferred cooking a native-style meal but with only Narku, my limited abilities and the wood stove, I did not feel confident. Narku bought the oysters at the *bung* and I added bacon from the cured roll in the fridge. The results were delicious; large rounds of fried bread, covered by thick rounds of butter-fried tender fillet steaks stuffed with oysters, covered with a spoon of hot Latvian liverwurst and served with slices of bacon, sweet potato and side plates of Chinese mushrooms and salads. Great platters of fresh local fruits followed – I could hear the guests slurping. Stan borrowed a generator so we had light if they stayed on, which of course they did. The guests were Australian engineers working on roads and bridges, and with the help of many bottles of our fine German wines, we played on into the night.

I had dragged out a cinnamon Thai-silk pintucked frock, tied my hair back with a gigantic pink satin bow and matching Italian high-heeled sandals. Ridiculous! I looked dressed for a mannequin parade not for slaving over the wood stove entertaining VIPs in a wooden shack, carrying in plates whilst hopping the holes in the floorboards. It was possibly my finest hour. Stan was proud of my efforts and so was I.

That night I learnt just how brilliant Stan was and how much Canberra thought of him. It was all pretty wondrous stuff but apart from cooking and smiling a lot, I could contribute nothing to the conversation. It was facts and figures and finally when they turned to me and said they hoped I would enjoy being a millionaire I gave them my very best smile and thanked God I hadn't spoken. The engineers said they would never forget that night.

We played Beethoven, Bach and Frank Sinatra on my battery-operated portable turntable. A Pole called Mick Kutz fell in love with me and stayed that way for years much to Stan's disgust, but I did occasionally feel obliged to ask Mick for dinner. He followed us to Moresby. He would bring his guitar and sing wonderful love songs and Stan would be shitty for days!

Next day while Narku and I were cleaning up, Stan (resting on one of the Comworks chairs drinking a rum-fizz!) explained what was happening. He was going to build large bridges as well as roads. He and a Sydney engineering company had merged and with the assistance of costing engineers in the company, intended tendering for a Markham Valley contract. This was a five-million-pound contract and he expected to win it because he knew the country, the weather and the equipment required to do the job.

He took the smile off my face by telling me he would be away for at least four months and I couldn't go with him because I would have to keep on working until he got on his feet. He also mentioned that he needed the 10,000 pounds I had in the bank to help towards the new equipment. I guess every girl should have a tractor in lieu of a glorybox! Then he said he would still be short but would go down to Comworks and play two-up and hopefully win. This he did, throwing in ten pounds initially and winning 4000, then throwing in that 4000 and losing. He started again and walked in for breakfast grinning and smelly and threw over 8000 pounds on the table. He suggested that I could try smiling!

I muttered around the house for a while hopping in an undignified, demented manner over the holes until finally he put his arms around me. Of course I was the usual melting minnie and he explained that this was my first test and he knew I wouldn't fail him. Actually I was under the impression I'd been tested constantly but I guess it's just the way we women look at things. I knew he was proud of me and that's all I needed. I sure was a simple girl!

The months to follow were a nightmare. I missed him so much and of course we couldn't phone or communicate at all.

One day, taking off for work in the jeep, there was a yell from

Stan Rybarz honoured by natives for opening up the Kumusi area for them by road and bridge. He was the first European to be given this distinction and their secret ceremonies and headcraft were bestowed upon him in appreciation.

The original church at Ryczow, where Stan
was christened

The church in 1975

Front of Stan's house, Ryczow,
with bullet holes still visible

My second home. Plantation type house, with garden of crotins and hibiscus

My fourth home, Port Moresby, while building Jackson Airport runway.
The home was surrounded by single-man *dongas*.

Polis Bois, Port Moresby

Beautiful Madang

Kumusi

Goroka *sing sing*

Goroka *sing sing*

Adelaide holidays. The Poles and the Germans become friends

Mother, Jane, Becky and me outside the Moresby house

Jane with her beloved dad building the Bridge together

Markham Road

Kumusi Bridge

Kumusi Bridge

Kumusi Bridge

Mt Lamington, at Popondetta, starting to erupt

Hibiscus flowers arranged on fronds

Sad farewell

Wau people dressed for partying

Busu River

behind some trees. I stopped to look and a *boi* jumped at the jeep and put his hand down my frock and grabbed my breast. Fortunately, I still had my foot on the accelerator so I jammed it down and lurched off. The office staff told me I looked ghastly and I think it was because I realised that I was acutely vulnerable.

We rigged up a bell that could be heard in Lucas's camp if trouble occurred again. Narku started driving me to work and collecting me. But I was now feeling insecure and Mary developed a nervous tic on her upper lip making it difficult for her to talk at all with her stutter and twitch. Oh, my goodness! We couldn't go out at night and return along the track in the jeep and Bekky had to be locked inside to protect her from harm.

I still managed to see Sheila and Ralph regularly. Ralph's jazz piano was just so good and Sheila was a soulmate. We could laugh till we ached like naughty school kids. I'll never forget when Sheila found Ralph's old diary. He had started writing Dear Diary in India where he met Sheila and fell madly in love with her. He invited her to visit his tea plantation in Ceylon and prior to her arrival he fantasised about her in the diary. Shiela and I had many girly giggly hours reading of Ralph's delicious heat searing through the pages. Darling Ralph, six foot nine inches tall and horny!

The months passed and Stan was finally due home. Mary stuttered that she would go and stay with Harold for a while. For the first time we had a substantial bank account and we felt encouraged. Stan told me, 'Pack bag for two and Bekky. We go Bulolo town with friends to big party.' As usual I did as I was told, rang Judith and Alan, and they joined us in the big diesel and we all set off up the winding mountain road. We stopped along the way to dunk in a beautiful natural pool and eat our Polish sausage and the native tomatoes and fresh fruit we picked on the way. I didn't want to leave this beautiful place.

Next we stopped near a thatched hut where native women

were weaving *bilum* bags resembling our shopping bags. The bags were about four feet square and made with reeds and were strong enough to carry a baby. A long band was attached to an opening and this band was worn across the forehead. The women huddled in darkened doorways and did not come to talk to us. I explained I wanted to buy a *bilum* and their attitude changed. There was great activity as they proudly showed me their wares, smiling and chattering to each other. They waved to us happily when we left for Bulolo with our purchases.

We arrived for the party. It was paid for by the Company and was for every one in the compound and their friends. The Americans knew how to treat their staff, and we had wonderful food flown in from Australia; plates loaded with fresh prawns, crayfish, turkeys and hams and southern fruit. And enough booze to start a hotel. Stan of course was monopolised by his old friends so Alan, Judy and I buddied up with a small visiting group and waited for the excellent band that was also flown in from Queensland by Bulolo Gold Dredging.

I had several dances with a chap called Denis who seemed to be following Stan's lead on the dance floor, and after a while I saw why. Stan was constantly dancing with a girl called Roma and at one stage, kissing her in a corner. Denis stiffened, looked at me and suggested we change partners. The other two were uncomfortable and both received the silent treatment from Denis and I until after the show. And everyone knew, except me, that Roma was the mother of a sturdy blond, blue-eyed, European-looking son. Next day, a shame-faced Roma eventually joined the breakfast party, with red-rimmed eyes that appeared to have been weeping copious tears all night. Denis and I raised our coffee cups to each other and twinkled into each other's eyes; I liked him very much. He stuck by Roma but he was no wimp. Stan was conspicuously silent.

Harold and I shared a love of the classics. One evening after listening to music and talking animatedly about Wagner, Stan could stand it no longer and interrupted saying, 'Excuse Bevvy – she make supper' and I was sent to the kitchen. At functions I was not allowed to dance with anyone. However if ships were in, Stan would allow me to dance with a sailor of his choice. This would be a bloke who could really dance and then of course I was supposed to shine on the floor.

I was at last beginning to understand the Polishman: a man's man who liked women who were admired (thus seen as a reflection of his good taste), not necessarily intelligent and preferably with few opinions. She needed to be ready and obliging for sex at all times, competent in the kitchen and not interfere when friends called. If these criteria were met, the world was her oyster. Most Poles are generous and loyal to their women, Stan was no exception. When money was in the bank I could have it all provided of course he actually handed it to me!

It was a man's world. There were no allowances made for women, no conveniences at all and only two Chinese trade stores. There were flesh-eating insects and tropical diseases. Both black and white males were kings. The black leaders were elected on the basis of wealth and bribery and helped by money from their ten wives! If I intended to assert myself, it would have to be done carefully.

I was also beginning to understand the role the Australian Government played in New Guinea. Australia had been nominated to educate the indigenous population and support them to independence. I believe we did a superb job with well-organised administrators who governed with intelligence and fairness. At all times the welfare of the New Guinea people was foremost. It was an enormous task. Many of the New Guineans felt their tribal powers would be in jeopardy necessitating tactful management.

Uniting New Guinea was a slow process. There were 856 distinct languages spoken and over 70 religious groups. The predominant language was Melanesian pidgin, followed by Police Motu and English. Pidgin was easy and adequate. A Chief Commissioner would be chosen to control a region. He in turn would employ District Officers, who would delegate to Patrol Officers. They had the dangerous job of entering all the villages, making themselves understood and hopefully introducing new laws and ideas. They then reported back to District Office. The Patrol Officers had no weapons but usually had two bearers who were both reliable interpreters. One of the bearers carried a shotgun for hunting food. Believe me, only men with guts survived in this job.

I suffered the tropical weather; northwest monsoons from December to March and southwest monsoons from May to October. Oh that humidity. But oh the beauty of luxurious rainforests, mountains unbelievably snow-capped on the peaks, delicate veils of cloud, wild orchids, variegated leaves and exquisite birds. There were crocodiles, snakes and spiders the size of plates and fascinating marsupials such as the cuscus, bandicoot, wallaby and tree kangaroo. I grew to know and love this rich and fascinating country.

As anticipated, we continued winning contracts in the Markham Valley. Stan's tender quotes were more competitive because he kept the company small. And it was clear his labour force respected him, in fact I think they would have died for him if requested.

On one occasion a large competitive company from Australia blocked an area with their equipment. When Stan realised he was unable to enter, he built a barge and ordered his *bois* to build pontoons and rafts, then loaded on his equipment and floated around, entering the area from the coast. I believe the exchanges were colourful on landing and the *bois* learned some Polish vocabulary that day! The natives turned on an improvised sing-sing when the last piece of equipment was landed. It went on all night and caused consternation and apprehension in the opposition camp. The native crew believed nobody could beat Taubada Stan.

Stan decided I should take a break from work again and join him in his working camp. District office had a capable relief worker and I wanted to see Stan's plans coming to fruition so joyfully Bek and I skipped to the plane that was to take me to my beloved. On arrival at the strip, we were jeeped to a river, transferred to a skimpy *lakatoi* (canoe), and taken miles upstream. I acquired a loathing of crocodiles from that moment but at least Bekky was happy as she felt she had found some playmates! We were then transferred to a massive D10 tractor and crawled slowly to my beloved. He wanted to take me to bed immediately but I had another plan that involved leaning over a large hole in the ground.

I learnt about landslides, quickly replaceable Bailey Bridges, equipment breakdowns and the advantage of locked brakes. I learnt about the slow ascent of mountains and the terrifyingly rapid descent. Being an animal lover, I really worked up an appetite when the local village had a pig kill! I lost a stone in weight and learned to love *kaukau* (sweet potatoes).

Everything was cooked in the ground under rocks and leaves, and sometimes the *line bois* would put on a *singsing* for *misis*. They wore wonderfully coloured headresses of red, blue and green parrot feathers or glorious bird of paradise feathers (I didn't ask what happened to the birds) and masses of beads, and the smell of pig fat rubbed on their bodies was strong. They were warm, generous people and we became firm friends.

Stan had planned a wonderful trip for me and we went to Kainantu, Goroka, and Kundiawa in the glorious Chimbu District.

The Chimbu reminded me of pictures of Switzerland and I was spellbound. There was a patchwork quilt of gardens on every available hillside. Mt. Wilhelm at 4509 metres is the highest mountain in the area and Kundiawa is the provincial capital. I could have done without the rafting on the Wahgi River, with its powerful rapids and waterfalls as the river wandered through deep chasms and under small rope bridges. As usual my dominant emotion was fear. I don't think my lips could move to scream and it was clear to me I had no natural affinity with this type of activity.

Goroka is an attractive town, shaded by lush green vegetation. It's the capital of the Eastern Highlands Province and Kainantu is the second-largest town. The most important river systems of PNG are here – the Ramu, Wahgi and Aure – and the climate is gorgeous with warm days and cool nights. With the perfume of frangipani in my nostrils, I watched the incredible Goroka mudmen dance. It depicted the attack on the village of Makehuku when many of the men were killed and the enemy carried off the women and children. One night the Makehuku men covered in grey river mud, silently danced into the village of their attackers, pretending they were the spirits of the murdered villagers. They wore clay masks with pig tusks, dog's teeth and shells and terrified their enemies who never attacked them again.

On leaving, they gave me one of their shooting arrows that I have cherished; five-pronged notches were for birds, metal prongs for fish and a single large prong for animals.

Kainantu situated between Lae and Goroka had been a coffee town, but cattle breeding had recently been introduced. I was uneasy about being there as the Kuru disease, unique to the area, was making headlines at the time. It was nicknamed the 'laughing disease' because the victims, who died about a year after showing the first symptoms, usually had a smile on their face at death. Subsequently it was found to be due to women and children eating the brain tissue of dead clan members. (There was a shortage of protein in some areas.)

We returned to the Markham camp and the massive river, the sixth largest in PNG. There are also dozens of short, fast rivers which added to the problems of road building as well as the swamps, earthquakes and lakes. The Markham Valley separates the Huon mountains from the Highlands and is a fault zone with regular earthquakes. An amazing thing had occurred and we couldn't believe our eyes. While we were away the river had completely changed course and Stan's bridges were standing proudly over nothing. What could we do but laugh and start again.

I found this holiday enthralling. I would go out with the crew in the morning, taking a book with me, but rarely reading one page. Instead I watched the gigantic equipment laboriously moving through the river and jungle, manned by our hardworking, determined operators, often bogged and in danger. It appeared surreal; man gradually forcing nature into accepting these huge constructions. Narku erected a covered tent area and the *bois* didn't mind me being there. I would help set up lunch and I asked many questions that I think they found flattering, and they in turn, I like to think, tried not to swear for my sake. At the end of the day and after another section completed, there was the hot dusty drive back to camp and cold beers and talk, usually about the progress made that day.

And so it went on, day after day. The road was finished that led to the river and then the bridge would be started. And then the bridge over the river and more road leading to smaller rivers and smaller bridges.

One day Stan suggested to *kuki boi* that he take me out to shoot lunch. I couldn't show that I was absolutely appalled at the thought. So away we went with a shotgun and Bekky in the jeep. Eventually I had to prove myself to *kuki boi* and I shot some poor

Here, and following pages: Markham Valley, building road and bridges

inoffensive half-starved bird with the longest neck I've ever seen. I could see *kuki boi* was happy I had bagged such a dreary dinner, and he didn't suggest we go shooting again. He did try not to smile too broadly when we found the bird as tough as a leather boot.

Sadly, I had to leave Stan and return to our little shack on the river knowing it was just a matter of time before we would be moving from Lae. The holiday had been a happy one for us both, although Stan had little time to spare. Stan told me we would be moving to Port Moresby in due course; he was going to work with another company on Jacksons Airport to gain airport experience, his new business was in good hands temporarily and my life, once again, was about to change.

A few weeks later I received a message from Stan bush-telegraph style. Mary and I were to make room for a friend of his called Bill Mac, and we were not to talk about him with anyone. Mary was nervously back (not by choice but because of Harold's insistence) and was too curious to miss out on this interesting visitor. Bill arrived; a handsome, charming and cultured man, and surprisingly formally dressed. Shiela and Ralph came around to help me with the entertaining and brought Shiela's workmate Zoe, who worked for an American oil company drilling in New Guinea. She was a hot little European mix and obviously hit the spot in more ways than one. As time and the partying went on, there were noticeable changes occurring with Bill. His dressing became more casual, he ate less and drank more. Zoe was off her brain in love and when they weren't drinking they were making love all over the house. It became disastrous with Bill acting like Jungle Jim. By the time Stan came home, Bill was a write-off.

Narku had come home with me and was wearing a long disap-proving face. Stan nudged him and in pigdin suggested too much 'nooky' was going on. Narku giggled and launched into a long pidgin discourse about what Bill had been up to – when vocabulary ran out, the conversation continued using charades.

Eventually Stan explained why Bill was with us and why we were hiding him. His sister was an important official with the United Nations who had come to New Guinea on United Nations business (probably to criticise Australia's efforts yet again). Bill had adopted a native lifestyle, living in a native village with his six wives. He had been one of the original Edie Creek gold miners and a good friend of the Leahy Brothers. Like Mick and Danny Leahy the gold he found made him fabulously wealthy but he didn't want to change his lifestyle. He asked Stan to hide him until his sister left. It all turned out okay in the end for everyone except Zoe who was invited to become wife number seven; sobbing she declined! It was becoming obvious that many of the blokes were setting up house with the *meris*. The Government was getting tougher, knowing that many of these women would be left without support, and eventually laws were put into place that protected the New Guineans.

Stan put the logging truck that he had lovingly built up for sale. People told me it was 'his baby' until I came on the scene. I used to sit in it up front near the winch as the massive logs rattled and swung perilously, and I envied no one. I did receive a few rude comments from the snobbier Lae community about this behaviour. However I had the last laugh later when one of Lae's socialites flew to Moresby to ask if we could bail her and her husband out of their monetary problems.

I also chuckled when Stan was invited to the opening of the Lae Golf Club. Up on stage he went as everyone gushed all over him and thanked him for building the Lae Golf Club. I thought the abovementioned lady had a sour expression especially when she spotted my exclusive Hartnell cocktail gown.

Lae Golf Club, which Stan helped to build

Lae was a sleepy and beautiful haven, a timeless tropical town. I loved it and in my mind I can still see the Japanese wreck the *Tenyo Maru* at the end of the airstrip half a mile off shore. I can hear the birdcalls and the crickets and I think I will always long to return.

As the population increased, so did the talent. I had mixed feelings about leaving Lae. It was delightful to live there and I had made some loyal friends. And some wild ones! I would classify our local doctor Tony as wild. He had a Greek and Maori background and was a frustrated classical pianist with enormous appetites in all directions. As a doctor he was reasonable. For a town inundated with skin rashes, itches and ulcers his classic answer to 'What can I do?' was 'Scratch it!' He was loud, generous, crude and kind, and sexy in a sweaty way. He was also massively overweight and had the habit of wiping the sweat off his heavy, handsome Maori features with his fingers, then sucking them. He played Beethoven with a passion and a certain degree of accuracy and I believe his lovemaking was somewhat the same! He often called in to see us at our 'yummy love nest' as he called it, and asked me if he could bring his current married love to the shack when I was at work. I said it was okay by me but I'd have to mention it to Stan, otherwise it could be misinterpreted (a worrying thought). But Stan was quite happy about Tonaks, as we called him, being there. He wouldn't have been so happy had he known how many times Tonaks had hit on me! Bella, his woman of the moment, was married to an airline captain who also enjoyed extra curricular activities. Bel was an extremely witty woman and her description of Tonaks perspiringly fornicating while humming Beethoven in time with each stroke was a treat to hear, particularly when she added that two cats jumped from the wardrobe on to his heaving shoulders during his noisy finale. He was so upset over this that he started yet another diet; this one the boiled egg diet. Everywhere he went he ate these eggs, and all our houses smelt of sulphur when he left.

As you can guess, affairs were common: small communities, heavy drinking, incessant heat and no house chores, led to idle time. I can remember Marj and Stu from Western Australia arriving; great looking people and fun company, he very wealthy and she an ex model. In no time at all gregarious Marj was filling in Stu's flying hours with Norman, who had a lucrative local trucking business. I was fascinated to learn that Norman had a penchant for being urinated upon during sex. These edifying titbits were enthralling! The golfcourse was used extensively for the preliminary courting and it boosted the membership no end.

The New Guinea people regarded this as reasonably normal, but they loved to drop little hints over the kitchen sink such as, '*Oooh – bigpela nem bilong Norman klostu!*' rolling their big brown eyes suggestively towards Marj's *donga*. There were no secrets in New Guinea!

Marj's *haus boi* adored her. Marj was sick one day, and I called over to offer help. I found Joseph sitting at her bedside while she was sleeping, holding her hand and looking at her lovingly. I don't believe he would ever have harmed her.

One of the more unusual affairs was a homosexual called Doug, renowned for his affairs with blokes, who fell madly in love with a scrawny woman called Annie. They had the most passionate affair culminating in marriage and ultimately children. Every now and then Doug would get shrieky and female and Annie would just say, 'Come here' and he'd go and grab her and kiss her, didn't matter where they were, and all would be quiet again.

Leaving Lae, I would miss the picture theatre under the stars with the mozzie machine belting out the spray and the babies covered with mosquito nets.

And the picnics on the Butibum River where we swung from the trees and laughed the day away, often wearing beer cartons instead of the forbidden bathing togs. We didn't 'skinnydip', that was looking for trouble. Or we would go across the Butibum to Wagan, a village near the black sand beach of Malahang, looking for driftwood.

No more visits to the Chinese shops where I could buy pretty well everything and if not, they'd get it for me. I can still see little Mrs Tommy Seeto, a baby each year (the youngest at the breast), and a pig tied to the sewing machine table as she made sheets, laplaps, mother hubbards and cooked the meals, all at the same time. And Mr Wan Jin Wah, who could add up and total before I had got to first base. It was hard for the New Guineans to accept the Chinese. They resented the Chinese because they were diligent and made money. The Chinese bought up many of the German plantations after the war, all of which made them wealthier. And they opened shops and trade stores all over New Guinea. They

Butibum River – our picnic and swimming spot

deserved their wealth but of course, the same rules applied to them as to all nonindigenous people; they only had 99-year leases. So it was all a gamble.

Our morals may not have been the best, but I don't believe this worked against our main role. We were kind and I believe patient as far as the native people were concerned. I believe we taught them much that was good.

There was a strange happening that I don't to this day understand. The Manager of Air Traffic Control invited us to a party of about 30 people at his home one Saturday before our departure. Late in the afternoon, someone pointed skywards to what appeared to be several cylindrical objects following a larger one. Alan the host called out to a guest with a camera to take a photograph, which he did, in fact he shot a roll. Some time later when Alan and his friend collected the film, there was a note of apology attached to say the film had been classified as security material and had been passed on to the appropriate Government office. Later we learnt that a Catholic priest had been shocked by rings of black burnt vegetation and flamed trees in the gardens of his manse damaged on the same day we had seen the cylinders. No explanation was offered.

On a more down to earth level, Harold had popped the question to deaf Mary. She was relieved to be out of our Milford Haven retreat and into Harold's flat. He suspected she had no intention of leaving so he proposed, she stuttered a 'Yes' and they lived happily ever after.

I had warned Burns Philp of my impending departure but it was still a few weeks before we were due to leave. I was sitting at my desk at 8.30 am when I felt the start of a headache. By 10 am it was raging and my temperature was at a dangerous level. They rushed me to hospital and that was the last thing I knew for over a week.

Gradually I became aware of sopping-wet sheets being repeatedly changed. Due to my careless approach to pill taking, I had a severe dose of malaria and suspected Blackwater Fever. My urine was black and I was terribly sick. The only bright spark in this debacle was I lost pounds in weight and looked pale and sort of pretty as I lay helpless on the hospital bed. Stan flew in and was concerned and caring – it was romantic. Anyway, I lived to tell the tale.

Stan insisted I give up work and get fit before leaving Lae. I found some gorgeous feral kittens born while I was away and of course fell in love with them. I managed to find homes for all except one – I pleaded with Stan to let me keep him. He agreed but said I had to 'deball it' before we took it to Moresby. That was a bit of a worry; we didn't have any vets in New Guinea! So I had a lesson in veterinary science: take a rusty razor blade, put the cat head-first in a bag and nick nick, they're gone, neat as a pin.

What was also amazing was that I did not make a sound while the operation was taking place. I had learnt over time that if I couldn't be brave at least I could be quiet and with any luck no one would notice. And, strangely, the kitten didn't seem too unhappy and lived a long and happy life. And Bekky had a friend again.

Bel was in financial trouble and was too scared to tell Gary. She was a good cook and came up with the idea of using my big wood stove to make meat pies to sell. It was actually a great idea and we could have made money as there was nothing similar in Lae. We worked flat out but still could not keep up with the orders. I cherish the memory of Stan's face on arriving home unexpectedly to find his lady covered in flour and his house in meat pies. Narku disapproved until Stan started to eat the produce at a great rate encouraging Narku to join him.

It was time to leave after three years in Lae. My much-loved turntable was packed away with the Jelly-Roll Morton records, saucepans and our personal belongings. I said tearful goodbyes to good friends, black and white, resigned my job, bequeathed the stove to Bella and away we went to Port Moresby.

I sat first class in a plane (without the cabbages) which felt strange. Bekky and Ras the cat were both upset at having to be boxed up to fly second class, instead of being able to wander around talking to the passengers. We were 'getting civilised' so the pets and pigs could no longer roam the plane.

In retrospect, I don't believe I have been happier than that time at Milford Haven and yet we had nothing in a material sense. As I reminisced I actually felt a little afraid at how it would be in

Port Moresby, the big metropolis. What had happened to that 'well brought up' person? Did she still exist after bush camps, violence, bad language, sex and rock and roll? I need not have worried. After all there had also been great beauty and tranquility in Lae and the jungle, and I was resilient.

Well Bek, Ras and I were off on another adventure, possibly the biggest yet. There would be a new home, a new job and new friends and I was soon to experience another culture shock: Port Moresby.

10

Port Moresby

We arrived at Jacksons Airport and the first thing that hit me was how it seemed less tropical and the vegetation appeared to be limited to spindly gum trees like an arid Australian town. The place was busy with people rushing around but the greatest surprise was that the car and not the jeep ruled the highways. We were back in civilisation for better or for worse.

Our compound was close to the airport and so barren I was shocked when I saw it. We drove up to our accommodation, the last and most elevated *donga* in a row of single and two-man *dongas*, and I remember feeling impressed that I had stairs to the wire front door and a proper shower. There were a few spindly trees near the compound's *haus kuk* that looked liked dying gum trees and not a palm tree to be seen!

There was roll call to greet us – talk about the League of Nations. There was a Canadian logger called Frank, a Bulgarian gutter specialist called Georgio Atanasov-Dobrazenski, Aussie/German Charlie the D10 operator, Janski a Czechoslovak trench-digger operator, Australians Steve and Tom, both carpenters, and Alfredo the Italian cement/terrazo specialist. Add to them a few Germans and a couple of Ukrainians, several more Italians, Russians, a Latvian and an Irishman plus 300 New Guinea and

Papuan *linebois* and I remember thinking there was a highly volatile cocktail ready for World War III. I felt like the Queen Mum being presented to 'the troops'.

We settled into our one bedroom home with lounge, kitchenette and shower. There were *pitpit* interior walls made from plaited reeds and an outside copper. The loo was outside of course and, inexplicably, to the left of the front door. The washing line hung from the toilet across the front of the *donga* to the workshop door. Certainly convenient! No landscape gardening here, just rows of heavy equipment and trucks all beautifully parked.

I wanted to get to work as soon as possible. Stan was talking marriage – something we hadn't ever discussed – but I wanted more time. I applied for a position as Confidential Secretary to the District Commissioner of the Central District of Papua, David Marsh. We liked each other instantly and I was employed to commence the next week. I soon learned that David was one of those

Accommodation, workshops, mess/cookhouse and earth moving equipment

rare beings; a truly great man. His humanity, compassion and integrity were an example to all who worked with him and we repaid him with our unstinting loyalty.

Stan worked long hours at the airstrip, whilst I became increasingly involved in the Australian administration of Papua New Guinea. It was a fascinating job. There was no national unity, in fact Papuans and New Guineans hated each other. There were tribal wars, as the natives trusted no one from another family or tribe. Basic education of these people had been primarily in the hands of the Catholic, Anglican, Lutheran and Seventh Day Adventist missionaries. Hygiene as we know it was unknown.

In the early 1950s, the responsibilities and workload of the District Commissioner and District Officers were immense. My job was also significant and demanding. Apart from the normal secretarial duties of shorthand, typing, and paperwork, I sat in the courthouse during land title claims. I had to type rapidly on an old Remington Manual, documenting everything spoken in pidgin English in the court. If there was dialect spoken, an interpreter translated into pigdin for me. Later I would retype the claims in English and then both pidgin and English copies would be attached for records.

The security files were another of my responsibilities. Everyone who came to work in New Guinea was screened before they arrived (some of them proved excellent liars). I updated their files as current information was received. This was serious stuff, as we didn't want troublemakers, political activists, religious fanatics or criminals of any kind. It was essential that the New Guinea people were treated with absolute respect, not used and abused in any way, nor politically or religiously manipulated. Any person caught breaking the rules was deported.

Our office issued all media statements, particularly to Rueters, and this was always challenging. We had the eyes of the world on us and all those watching were ready and waiting to criticise our every move. Misquotes, an 'off the cuff' statement or inacurate facts and we paid for it with stinging criticism from around the world.

David organised Badi, a trainee journalist, to visit native villages with our Patrol Officers and write reports of the conditions in the villages. Our office would then analyse this information and plan improvements based on Badi's excellent work. It was a simple, effective system that followed the 'hasten slowly' approach. Imagine how exciting it was when we sent a New Guinea primary school teacher with a nurse and hygienist to set up in a village, taking with them our gift of their first sewing machine.

On the home front, I put up the curtains! I also enamelled old cane chairs in vivid colours, and talked kindly to the wood stove and the carpet snake in the toilet, both of which were benign but noisy, the latter crunching his dinner rat all night.

Every morning there was rollcall in the compound. Stan would rapidly give out the day's instructions in Motu (an Austronesian language), pidgin and English. He knew the names of the 300 *bois* employed and they would grin with pride if he made a comment to them. Then the equipment would start to roll – oh the dust – oh my sinuses! There were huge tractors, turnapulls and graders, and about 30 trucks, all bright yellow. One thing I learnt very quickly – never walk near any of the *bois* as they cleared their sinuses; you wore it!

We began to socialise. Stan, with his original Polish friends from Rabaul who had come to join him, had many noisy argumentative evenings playing chess or cards. The night usually culminated in the cards or pawns being thrown everywhere. As our bedroom was off the lounge, I lived a sleepless life. I found the Poles worked hard, played hard, screwed hard, fought hard and I believe were probably the most difficult but proudest people in Europe. It never occurred to them or Stan that I might get tired of their constant visits disturbing my rest. They intruded dreadfully but I was diplomatic and said nothing!

Both Stefan and Louis had suffered terribly for years as Russian prisoners in Siberia. Louis showed me a chess set he made during this time by picking up any piece of paper he found in the prison, fashioning it into papier mâché and eventually moulding chess figures. It was a work of art.

Poor Billy was in a terrible way; he was on a full British pension and Stan warned me that he had been shattered with gunshot wounds and was mentally unstable. He explained that Billy could become 'a little strange' but he hoped I would be kind. Well! I remember the first time Billy was 'strange'. We were sitting around the cane table when he jumped up, rushed behind the fridge and rat-a-tat-tatted with an imaginery machine gun. He then ran into the bedroom and hid behind the bed, screaming in Polish and throwing himself all over the floor. I nearly had a heart attack! Stan quietened Billy down with straight vodka! Everyone just sat there as if nothing had happened and it was of no interest that I was shaking like a leaf.

Another interesting character to join us was Paddy O'Riordan – another colourful Irishman. Dear Paddy with his generous heart was the most incompetent person I have ever known. I just loved him and his blarney was delightful. Even Stan put up with his antics.

One morning Stan decided to give Paddy a chance on one of the big machines. Stan moved the machine to the workshop block on the opposite side of the road and explained to a very excited Paddy he was to level the block. We did a very silly thing – we forgot him. But darling Paddy did what was asked of him – he went up and down until he dug a deep swimming pool! All Stan could think of doing was throwing his bandana on the ground and stamping on it! We had a major exercise then to crane the big machine out, the labour cost was enormous, and in the excitement Paddy lost his false teeth. Gummily he told me it didn't matter because he ate with his hands and never chewed anything. It was true. I eventually witnessed Paddy eating stew from a bowl with his hands.

Our day started at 5 am. I would get up before Stan and light the wood stove which I had set the night before, and then start cooking breakfast. Then he would get up and plan his roster for the day, open up the various workshops, check things out and return for breakfast.

Each morning as I worked on the bench I would see a *boi* standing in front of my kitchen playing with himself. It really wasn't a good start to my day. I mean it's difficult to ignore a chronic masturbator at any hour let alone at five o'clock in the morning. Finally I complained to Stan and he said either I was imagining it or it was wishful thinking! I was so indignant I woke Stan up earlier than usual next morning, made him crawl without being seen to the cooking area, and waited for the lad to commence proceedings. I felt somewhat smug when Stan roared out of the *donga* in hot pursuit of this poor little bloke, now naked having lost his *laplap*, his penis wagging in the breeze. Actually, for a gal who had been brought up with no display of genitalia in her life, I quite enjoyed seeing all the types and sizes shown around the camp.

Stan called the roll and I found myself covering my mouth so they couldn't hear my shrieks of delight as Stan attempted to explain with appropriate gestures to 500 *line bois*, that they weren't to wank in front of *misis*. He was purple in the face and wriggling with discomfort as we ate our breakfast in silence.

Our lifestyle was basic. My dear mother came up for Christmas and could not believe that the men didn't stand up when she entered a room. In fact they were sitting on her bed behind the hallway door while she stood waiting for a chair that was never forthcoming. It was shock after shock for the old dear. She had simply never met anyone like Stan in her life and the heat from the wood stove didn't help; no airconditioning in those days. And then of course the carpet snake in the toilet caused the never-ending petulant question, 'What is that strange noise in the toilet?' We never did tell her. I like to think she enjoyed her holiday. We sent her off on the tourist bit around Papua New Guinea when our little nest was becoming too much for her and oh the tales she could tell on returning to Adelaide. And eventually, like everyone, she came to like and respect my Polishman.

So many interesting people came up on contract. Gentleman Tony from Rocla Pipes was a happily married man and devoted father of three, who gratefully accepted our invitations to dinner as he missed his home so much. He frequently visited our *donga* until Stan started showing resentment and Tony wisely decided he should limit his visits.

Stan brought another chap home called David. He was a whiz at English history, an absolute fanatic, and he and Stan would have many interesting debates. Stan liked him but David was deported for being a 'peeping Tom'; he used to perve on the nurses quarters. We missed his talks whilst he was languishing in gaol.

As the only woman in the camp I did have to show caution although I found it difficult to conform to what was considered proper behaviour.

For example, one of our carpenters was an excellent worker but an alcoholic. One night, a bit under the weather, he firmly rebuked Stan for speaking to me 'without due respect'. Stan's face was a study; he was so shocked at this scrawny little guy having the guts to tell him off, he actually thanked him for his concern. I thought it wise not to comment! Then there was Alfredo, our harmless Italian tile layer, who clutching a bottle of Italian wine, serenaded me from a paw-paw tree. He chose nights when Stan was away until the night that he made a mistake. Stan mumbled to me in bed, 'What dat noise?' He had a quiet word with Alfredo next morning and I was not serenaded for a while.

Macky, one of the Irish boys, suffered badly from sunburn. He had a round map-of-Ireland face, covered at all times with white calamine lotion, and bright carrot-coloured hair. He loved his rum and every time he got drunk he'd weave bow-legged around the compound telling everyone that I should become a nun because God had given me the face of an angel. He also suffered from haemorrhoids and would scratch his rear end as he walked along on his bandy legs.

One night, I awoke to wierd thumping noises. Waking Stan I asked if he would see what was going on. He was evasive which made me suspicious so I put on a frock and went around the corner to the sleeping quarters only to find the *bois* copulating. Subdued I returned to bed and Stan fortunately, did not comment. It was difficult not to be preoccupied with these strange behaviours.

There was a worrying side to all this. We Australians were there ostensibly to train the Papua New Guinea people and educate them to self-government. We apprenticed them and taught them a trade but in doing so, we took away the security of village life. In industry it was sometimes difficult to provide married accommodation, forcing the men to share sleeping quarters. This of course was an unnatural way for the lads to live. The Salvation Army was brilliant as usual building transit houses so the *meris* could come and stay for short periods and bring the children. A bowl of nourishing soup, bread and fruit was provided free of charge each day, and this certainly helped families stay together. I feel privileged to have come from an Army family and to have so often witnessed the remarkable practical work of these people.

One night Peggy's husband John, who was Director of Posts and Telegraphs, and his brother Peter, who was visiting from Sydney, came around for dinner. Stan was away and my friend Peg was in Australia adopting their second child. Lamb that had arrived on the ship that week was cooked as a celebratory treat, and candles and fine Spanish wine had been placed on the table. We had just sat down to dinner when the front door burst open and a wild-eyed apparition dragged the startled Peter by the collar and threw him out the door. It was my Polish darlinka who had unexpectedly arrived home and as usual thought the worst when he saw an unknown car and heard a male voice. Candles and food fell off the table some landing on John who had not as yet been noticed by Stan.

What could I do? John was livid. With a sombre voice he suggested Stan find a brain. He then went outside to pick up his poor quivering brother who by this time was surrounded by *bois* offering help but failing to alleviate his fear. I could hear him muttering in a shaking voice that John hadn't told him about a mad Russian and I had that irresistible urge to giggle when I saw Stan's face; being called a mad Russian was the last straw! Eventually apologies were given and accepted, but the night was ruined. It would make a good tale for Peter when he returned south. Suggesting that Stan inform us all when he was coming home went down like a lead balloon. He made his own rules.

For Sunday morning brunch we sometimes went to the RSL club on the Ela beachfront. One Sunday morning a group of us were sitting around a table eating and without thinking I asked Stan to stop tapping his foot on mine because it was irritating. Well the 'shit hit the fan' as the saying goes; up and over went the table with a dozen bacon and eggs and coffees and some poor unfortunate fellow whom I didn't know and never saw again was up-ended and thrown out on the lawn. I heard someone who obviously had a hangover say, 'Who's making that fucking noise?' Nobody, least of all me, really knew what was happening but we did look stupid with bacon and eggs dripping down our frocks and shirts. I bet that young man thought twice before playing footsies under the table again.

Another Sunday morning I was entertaining friends for 'elevenses' as we called them. This usually consisted of rum swizzles with Angels on Horseback (prunes or local oysters wrapped in bacon). A rum swizzle comprised 100 per cent overproof rum with sugar around the top of the glass and very little ginger ale. There was a rattle of the wire door and as I opened it I felt the sharp jab of a 303 rifle shoved into my stomach and a rough voice asked, 'Where's Abe?' The smile left my face, my body froze and my guests were definitely not coming to my aid. I managed a faint, 'Who's Abe?' and was pulled down the stairs and walked across the compound to the mess hall with the gun in my back. Arriving at the mess on a Sunday morning was not an enriching experience; the hungover crew did not smell like rosebuds and they hated the world including the boss's wife. And in my opinion it took them far too long to blearily realise I was connected to the end of a 303. Perhaps they were savouring the moment?

Our fellow seemed to feel at home. He sat down and ordered a coffee still toting the gun. It appeared that Abe had absconded with this very angry man's wife from Wewak and had purportedly arrived at our compound. Fortunately the cuckolded husband believed us when we said we hadn't seen Abe. When Mike Thomas our Inspector of Police arrived at the compound (yet again) to investigate the problem he gave me a knowing look as he took the bloke away. I know Mike was wondering how I would explain this to Stan. Imagine how we all aged when Tom the carpenter opened the toilet door and guess who was hiding there? Yes, the happy runaways!

As for Stan, I guess turning purple in the face was a sign he was not a happy hubby, and of course it was entirely my fault! I reminded him that had he been home on a Sunday morning as other husbands were, instead of in the workshop, I might not have ended up at the point of a gun! And I mumblingly called him a *duzy niedzwiedzia*, (in English, 'big bear') in my favourite affectionate way so it sounded like doozynichwich.

Fortunately Stan and David Marsh respected and liked each other so I had wholehearted encouragement regarding work. However problems were developing in Port Moresby town and to a lesser degree in the bush. A couple of ignorant left-wing politicians came up from South Australia and held a public meeting. They talked to the Moresby indigenous population, sanctimoniously called them brothers, stirred them up about something called a trade union and then left us to cope. This was frustrating for District Office. How on earth could we explain unions to approximately two million people who were still using bows and arrows in most of the villages, whose land was valued in group ownership, and whose chiefs followed tradition not progress? Anyway we did our best but it seemed far too early for this to occur. Obviously the politicians just wanted a story so they would look important for the southern newspapers. It didn't matter to them that the native people were left upset and confused adding to potentially serious problems which were developing in West New Guinea (previously Dutch New Guinea), Timor and Bougainville.

The aftermath of this thoughtlessness that left the locals agitated, occurred the following afternoon at a public *singsing* held on a sports oval. Pam Kirke, her two children and I decided to attend and were enjoying the rich harmonies until a Papuan *boi* made a pass at a New Guinea *meri*. Silence fell and we felt fear. Pam looked at me and hissed, 'Let's move!' I picked up one child and she the other and we ran to our jeep. Others were doing the same. We drove around to David's home and told him what was happening and he went straight to the oval and walked through the melee alone without a weapon and calmed everyone in a few minutes. For hours we heard eerie banging on the electricity poles throughout the town. We lay awake and frightened through the night as the Kundu drums played. It was dangerous to be out. Irish Paddy got caught in town and was beaten badly.

Papua New Guinea was a magnet for the religiously zealous who sometimes lied about their religious commitments during the screening process. Once settled, they preached a contradictory doctrine to those established. The first white man murdered by a native was a church minister, killed due to a fight between two religious factions. Problems were caused by a Seventh Day Adventist church holding services on Saturdays not Sundays, while another church believed it a sin.

I was furious when a Russian and Indian delegation from the United Nations reported that we had racially segregated beaches. They were sexually segregated. The beaches had signs up to protect the native people. They would get sexually aroused at seeing the legs of the Australian girls in swimmers. The native girls were usually bare breasted so this was no big deal, but display of legs normally hidden under skirts was stimulating. Some poor *boi* could end up on a charge and I dare to say now a few white-skinned girls would have missed a heartbeat seeing the superbly built native males nuding it through Ela Beach! David wisely decided rather than stop everyone swimming, we would swim at different times.

The Russians also queried why we hadn't changed the law that prohibited the New Guinea people drinking alcohol. Despite international pressure, David insisted the law remain for the protection of the native people. We had enough trouble with the whites drinking in the heat!

Fortunately my administration job gave me a needed respite

from my male-dominated living quarters. I lived with a contractor who worked all over Papua New Guinea. It was a man's world; dirty, crude, boozy, and lecherous. However it enabled me to see the big picture, which was useful in my job. Our workers had absolutely no respect for women but both black and white males worked well together and I would sometimes look out with wonder and watch them working late at night under lights to finish a job without necessarily incurring penalty rates. They respected Stan who treated them fairly and they repaid him by working their guts out.

I was beginning to enjoy Port Moresby. It had a large and varied population, the biggest in the Territory, of about 30,000 native people and 15,000 Europeans. It was a sprawling town with personality and character.

Many different tribal groups settled in Moresby looking for work. Initially there had been two main groups, the Motu and the Koitabu. The Motu were great sailors with 15-metre-long *lakatois* (boats) and villages built on stilts over Moresby Harbour. Hanuabada, one of six interlinked villages, is the original great village of stilt houses and I was fortunate to spend some time there and meet the people. It was explained to me that invitations must be extended from the Hanuabadans to visit. To wander uninvited around the walkways was an intrusion of their privacy.

On the southern side of town is Ela Beach, then Koki Market, Boroko (often called Four Mile) and Seven Mile where I lived. Then the road divides north to the Brown River and east to the mountains, the Kokoda Trail and Sogeri.

Sogeri is only 46 km from Moresby and the Bomana War Cemetery is just past the turn-off. We always spent a sobering Anzac morning at Bomana. Black and white joined in friendship and sorrow, tears pouring down all our faces! A few kilometres past

Hanuaban house on stilts in the water

the cemetery the road winds up the Laloki River gorge, to the spectacular Rouna Falls, a wonderful cool spot to relax, forget the heat of Moresby and perhaps take a dip in the Crystal Rapids.

We made many escapes from the incessant heat; to Lake Sirinumu near Sogeri, one of the largest lakes in Papua New Guinea, and Brown River through the teak plantations. Loloata Island in Bootless Bay, and Tubusereia, Gaire, Gaba Gaba, Rigo, and Kwikila were all cooler places to visit when we could get away.

David suggested I visit Bereina on Yule Island and stay at the Carmelite convent that had been the base for the first Catholic Missionaries. Papua New Guinea's recent history is very much intertwined with the missions. The London Missionary Society and the Seventh-Day Adventists had extensive influence, and education was predominantly in the hands of Catholic, Anglican and Lutheran missions.

I met the Mekeo people of the area with their clever geometric face painting and colourful dancing costumes and I visited Kairuku the main village on the island.

And certainly an experience that to this day makes me shiver, is takeoff from the airstrip at Wau. It was built into a hillside and ran steeply down hill, with a sheer drop at the end. Take-off was a choice of flying or falling.

We survived to return to Moresby and the appalling traffic and appalling driving. At noon and at 5 pm it was bedlam with police officers waving hands hysterically, horns tooting on overloaded trucks with merchandise haphazardly packed, workers crammed up like sardines in a tin singing happily, all stalled in traffic jams. Buses ran but were totally unreliable – it was quicker walking.

Saturday mornings were fun in town as the police band marched through the shopping area playing bagpipes. Dressed in black edged *laplaps* and berets they looked smart and played well causing shoppers to march, not walk, whilst shopping. Generally speaking, the police were efficient despite not being permitted to carry weapons, and law and order was maintained. Their boss was our aforementioned English friend Inspector Mike Thomas, a good officer and a man of integrity respected by all. He applied British standards of law and order with a certain amount of pomp and splendour that appealed tremendously to the New Guinea people.

It was common practice to visit the native market, the *bung*, on Saturday mornings and barter for the fresh local fruit and vegetables and particularly the fresh fish. This helped to vary the otherwise monotonous food, although *bulmakau* (cattle) had just been introduced, and deer were already in the Brown River area.

Shooting deer turned out to be a bit of a problem. Initially many of the shooters got lost and in some cases were never found. The Brown River was a weird place and the story circulated that the shooters 'made a very fine stew'.

Life was never dull. Our compound was situated next door to a lady of enormous proportions called Catie who weighed 25 stone and owned a crocodile for a pet. Her garden *boi* raped her. Now that was brave but getting past the crocodile was braver. At the amazing courtcase he said it was worth it: '*Bigpela misis namba wan fuk fuk – gutpela!*'

Stan said that he made me grow up and even though I was indignant at the time, he was quite right. I did have to cope on my own most of the time and Adelaide seemed a long way away.

Stan was in the workshop areas one morning when I heard a bad moaning noise. I looked out through my front window and it seemed that a *boi* was in trouble under a jeep. No one was around so I went over. What a scene! The Papuan had been working on his jeep when it seemed a live electricity wire hanging from a tree had landed on the jeep and then on his stomach and he was literally being frizzed alive. I rushed around like an idiot as the *boi* lay dying in front of me. I remembered Stan saying once about using wood if there was no rubber around so I grabbed a wooden-handled spade and threw it at the wire. Surprisingly I did not kill the Papuan and it safely knocked the wire off. The poor bloke rolled his eyes at me, and I felt guilty at having extended his suffering through ignorance. I ran to the workshop and Stan gathered from my gabbling that something was probably wrong and later even though he ticked me off for the way I coped, I sensed he was not totally displeased with me. I think in reality, I was always on trial. The poor bloke was flown south and lived, although I heard he was a bit 'fused together'.

As the months rolled on Stan started pricing tenders in his new company name as the airport tarmac was nearing completion. We were excited at our new status.

As I hadn't been to Madang, I took a few days off from the office and combined work with pleasure by joining him there. I had to travel by cargo plane in amongst the cabbages again but it was worth it. Madang is a delightful town with attractive cocoa plantations providing the necessary income. The town is perched on a peninsula jutting out into the sea and is liberally sprinkled with ponds, waterways and perfect islands. It reminded me of Venice. I have heard claims it's the most beautiful town in the whole country. I love Russian biologist Nicolai Miklouho-Maclay's description of the islands in Madang Harbour as, 'The Archipelago of Contented Men'. I became intrigued with the pottery of the region; it reminded me of terracotta. The potters tossed a stone into a ball of clay until it became a round pot. They then worked the outer surface with their hands and beat the clay with sticks before firing and decorated it with striking traditional village drawings that I found absolutely fascinating.

I was to get to know Madang very well. There was so much to be done there; roads and bridges were the Administration's first priority and Stan won tenders. Madang was virtually demolished during the war and had to be rebuilt, and infrastructure was needed in the Ramu Valley to support this new cattle-and-sugar-producing centre of New Guinea.

Whilst in romantic Madang, Stan and I decided it was time to marry and start a family. He told me that he wanted me with him and I would have to leave my job (which was going to be an incredible wrench) and follow him around the country. I wasn't too happy about this, principally because I would have so little to do. The thought of just being the cook for the camp did not appeal.

We also intended going south for a couple of months to

The airline office

introduce Stan to my family and get out of the tropics for a time.
There were two unspoken Administration rules: never drink
alcohol before 4 pm and holiday south every 21 months. Both of
these policies helped stabilise us and saved us from 'going troppo'
(I think).

I couldn't help wondering how the conservative 'rellies' would
rate Stan. At least they wouldn't see him with bare feet in his
tight-fitting working shorts wearing a handkerchief knotted
on each corner on his head, swearing in his loud guttural voice.
I hadn't seen him dressed southern style so that was quite an
intriguing thought.

Back in Port Moresby I commenced wedding planning. Shiela
was to be my matron of honour and Ralph would play piano at the
reception. As the Poles refused to come to the wedding *unless* it
was Catholic, and my family wouldn't speak to either of us if it *was*

Catholic, we arranged a joint Catholic/ Anglican wedding in the Taurama Army Barracks church. We made both priests promise they wouldn't drink until after the wedding. They were friends but once they were no longer sober fighting was inevitable. I planned toasts at the very snobby Koitaki Club and partying overnight at the Sogeri Hotel in wealthy rubber/copra plantation country. I booked Sheila and Ralph to stay at the hotel with us. They would enjoy spending a couple of days seeing the glorious scenery and awesome waterfalls before returning to Lae.

So everything was teed up and I was radiant with expectation. And then of course we had a little drama that took the smile right off my face. I stepped on some kittens on our front doorstep leaving them decidedly thinner. Stan asked me what I intended to do with them and I hadn't the slightest idea. Of course I was told I had to destroy them, without help, leaving me a neurotic mess for weeks. I slept outside the mosquito net until Stan was leaving for the bush; the mozzies buzzed with happiness, I itched, and Stan sulked in Polish. I really did have to learn the hard way! Subsequently we had a death adder on the second step to the front door. I hate to admit it but I didn't kill this snake – nor did I tell Stan. I just frightened it away and didn't admit I was a coward.

I spoke to David about the forthcoming marriage and he was pleased for me but sad that I would be going. However a date hadn't been set so we continued with plans for me to visit more villages and my schooling in the idiosyncrasies of the area, one of which was the greeting given to strangers. This demanded I stand very still while the native people felt all over my body – up the skirts, down the cleavage. When the moment came I must admit I was a little embarrassed but they were generous people and didn't seem to mind and sat me down to a feast of sago and wild pig in the Long Haus, which meant I had been accepted. What a rich variety of experiences I was lucky enough to enjoy.

Material things simply didn't matter. Money was a silver coin with a hole in the middle minted in New Guinea and valued about 10 cents but the indigenous people worked out their own bartering system, sometimes pigs, sometimes shells, and it appeared to work well.

Amazingly, the more Stan roared at the *linebois* the more love and respect he received. I still remember the day Stan was called to the Kiap office and told he was not to swear at the *bois* and if he broke the rule, they would revoke his licence to employ. This meant the end of his business. Take his working *bois* away from him and there were no contracts. No contracts, no Rybarz Contractors. So I had many a private chuckle listening to Stan roaring, 'You jolly donkeys'.

The wedding date was set for 31 August 1957. When the day arrived, I was bedecked in the appropriate bouffant frock and frangipani, Stan handsome in a white tropical dinner suit. The Taurama chapel was a charming native-style building with *pitpit* walls and the whole of Moresby seemed to be there. They all followed us up the mountains to Sogeri and stayed with us – what a wedding! Ralph played his wonderful piano and Stan and I were pretty darn happy. When we finally went to bed, we discovered the bed was full of snakes – a little joke from our working crew! Next day we all adjourned to the Koitaki Club and many of the members thought they were being invaded from outer space; our working crew *were* a bit different! And Stan by raising his voice a couple of octaves and using a few colourful phrases managed to empty the bar in less than a half an hour. I was used to this by now, but I did suggest he could perhaps tone things down a bit. His answer was predictable; he commented loudly where his donations to the club could be shoved! It seems millionaires really can do what they like.

Harry Wilson, me and Stan

Shiela

Mavis Mathieson and me, outside the charming chapel with *pitpit* walls and thatched roof

Ralph and me

We settled back in Moresby. Stan planned to move his head office to Popondetta, so some of his workshops had to be dismantled. One day an altercation occurred between Hanuabadan and Iduabadan *bois*. Stan walked into the midst without a weapon, knocked their heads together and while they were reeling around, mimicked them and made everyone laugh. This moment saved the business from a lot of pain! It didn't take much to start a riot with such fundamental differences between villages.

The European crew also created their share of worries. I repeatedly heard strange creaking noises under our *donga* at night and eventually braved the snakes to have a look. There were detonators and gelignite everywhere, obviously stolen, and what was worse, obviously stolen for a reason. I told Stan I thought it was Charlie the operator. After all he had walked out of the Boroka Hotel with a table and four chairs in the mid-afternoon and presented them to us for a wedding present. We actually received everything from dinner settings to salt and pepper sets all stamped Boroka Hotel underneath. Of course all had to be returned and Stan came to an arrangement with the proprietors not to involve the police. Charlie was indignant and told me it was the thought that counted.

Charlie and friends *were* the culprits regarding the gelignite and detonators – they were going fishing, illegally 'blowing fish'. I won points from this incident though, for not going to the police, and was rewarded with the crew's loyalty when we were in the bush.

The Italian operators also gave us a few problems. They pursued the native girls with great Latin passion. The girls fell pregnant and were locked in the men's *dongas* when the babies were due. This would stop any claims for maintenance from the villagers, but it put us in a very awkward position as the administration had stringent rules about the care and support of the little ones.

The yowling of the poor *meri* in labour would go on all night and left us all looking like twisted sandshoes next day. Stan had to threaten sackings to get this under control but eventually we had law and order in the compound. It did however remain common practice in the bush for some time, until the administration really got tough and introduced gaol sentences.

Generally speaking we all got on well but sometimes frightening things happened. My friend Peg organised a pre-wedding afternoon tea party for a mutual friend. We were waiting for one more lass to arrive and she did so, scraping at the front door on her knees, with her throat cut. It was a ghastly sight. She had argued with her *hausboi* and he took to her with his trusty-rusty knife. She survived but didn't talk much for a while. We all wobbled home with the help of many gin tonics taking the warning very much to heart.

During the mid-fifties, the United Nations was pressing for equality and for the New Guinea people to have self-determination as soon as possible. We all knew this was premature and felt the native people were not ready but we were forced to hurry the process. How could we give independence to people who were still dressed in feathers and leaves? I felt it would be a crime. David Marsh was furious and worried that we had to give approval for the native consumption of alcohol. He had always said it would do great harm to the people he loved so much and ultimately he was right.

Sadly we all ended up feeling insecure for a while. I can remember waking up yet another night hearing something unusual. Stan was out bush so I grabbed an axe and went outside to look around. All of a sudden I came face to face with someone wielding a big *sarap* (knife) just about to come at me. It was Joseph, one of Stan's mechanics who'd also heard something and was going to 'save the *misis*'. I don't know who was more scared Joseph or I. The prowler got away.

I had to start packing ready to close up my little *donga*. I had written to Max Harris of Mary Martin's Bookshop in Adelaide and told him I would be going bush and needed plenty of good reading matter. He sent a variety of excellent books, the first of many collections that I believe helped to keep me sane in the years to come. My first trip was to the Sepik.

11

Sepik River

I started what was to become a very frightening journey. Our head office had been moved to Popondetta and Stan had already commenced his first bridge there. But I was to join him at the Sepik River where he was looking over bridge sites for his new contract. The trip had been organised with some of his crew escorting me. One of his trusted mechanics told me proudly that the Sepik people had been headhunters and not cannibals because there was so much fish that they never acquired a taste for meat. I was so happy when he told me that; to know I could lose my head but it wouldn't be in the weekend stew made a world of difference. The town of Telefomin was well known for its residents' gourmet tastes and after hastily checking my map I felt somewhat relieved that it was some many mountains away from our camp, definitely too far for a quick takeaway.

Off we went to the airport, our destination a town called Angoram. From there we were to travel up river in motorised canoes, stopping at various trading posts and alternating with land transport where practicable. After walking down Tobacco Road, the main track of Angoram, Bekky and I thought the sooner we left the heat and the mosquitoes the better. How could I have thought we would leave them? After a very uncomfortable but I must stress hospitable night at the administration office we took off to my darling Polishman. How much in love can a woman be? I can remember telling Stan I would be with him wherever, but I was beginning to think I had been a bit rash!

We set off very early next morning and Bekky perked up no end. Being an English setter she was the true water dog. She barked at every *pukpuk* (crocodile), and the *bois* were most impressed. Personally I was stupefied and sick with fear, my stomach eddying with the river. The crew chatted away informing me of the many boats and passengers that had been lost on this river and I contributed to the chat by 'chucking' overboard at regular intervals. Bekky was so excited there was the distinct probability we would be next in the river. It was a total waste of time telling her to settle down. The way things were going the crocs would do that for her. I came to the conclusion that dying could be preferable.

The *bois* informed me we were stopping overnight so we pulled in through a *barad* (waterway) and to my amazement there were houses on posts about five feet above the channel. This was because there was literally no land. These people had floating gardens. The wild sugar cane called *pitpit* would often break away from the mainland and become an island, that when established was attached to a house and became a garden. If you were cheeky enough you could steal it during the night.

We spent an uncomfortable night in a strange spindly structure; the *haus kiap*. This was one of many buildings occupied by the New Guinea administration. There was one large room with a fire in the centre and cooking appliances all around. The floor was made of split sago bark and not at all strong. All cooking was done on this fire and the room was very smelly – great for my stomach! At least we towered over the crocs and it was safe to sleep.

The women avoided my eyes and did not speak until we were

leaving. I think they were just shy and perhaps a little wary, or perhaps I just smelt. There were gifts in another boat for the *meris* and *mankis* (young boys) such as lollywater (aerated water), lengths of material and salt, a very important commodity. Beads, combs, sweets, footballs, yo-yos and singlet tops were also acceptable. When we left the women were showing my gifts with pride and at last they smiled shyly at me.

The crew intended travelling all day and somehow I began to cope a little better. I actually started to believe we might still be alive to make another stop, minus our skin. The mosquitoes were almost unendurable and as there wasn't much else we could do, we double dosed with our malaria pills and painted ourselves with calomine lotion.

We visited another village, a little cleaner and more attractive than the last, and saw some Sepik mask and figurine carvings, distinctively painted with vegetable dyes or earth colours. Lime was used for white, ground ochre was mixed with sap for red and charcoal blended with oil for black.

Our journey continued over shallow lakes, with vegetation varying from tall *pitpit* to swampland with water lilies, which I was told not to touch as the crocs were sheltered underneath the leaves. I'm sure it was beautiful but the only thing I wanted to see was land with Stan standing firmly on it. I was assured it wouldn't be too long before we reached our destination. We spent another night in a *haus kiap*. This one was relatively comfortable but hot one minute and damp and chilly the next. We were told that Stan was to undergo a special ceremony when we arrived at his camp and I couldn't help feebly wondering if we were to be the ceremony, perhaps in a cooking pot!

After four long days, the big day arrived at last, and I cried when I saw the big Polak waiting at the river's edge. I fell out of the boat and into his arms and the *bois* all cheered us as we devoured each other. What a sight I was, unwashed with matted hair and probably irreversible gum disease!

At the camp the familiar sights of a jetty, a road, trucks and tractors helped me feel at home. I subsequently learnt that much of Stan's equipment was brought down the river on native-made pontoons and why weather was so important when tendering for a contract. The wet season was impossible. The equipment had to be appropriate for the terrain and fuel, fresh water and food had to be considered for a successful tender.

Stan had made camp close to the village of Kanganaman and it was here that a ceremony honouring Stan was to take place in the place where the spirits lived; the Haus Tambaran. This was strictly for men although they occassionally, begrudgingly, allowed white women inside. However I had no intention of upsetting the spirits. Indigenous women weren't even allowed to walk past and it could mean death if they broke the rules. I was so fragile I happily stayed with the girls. The ceremony commenced and there was great yelling and once again I couldn't help wondering if Stan was being feted or eaten. However he was being acknowledged as *namba wan wantok* (great friend) and was carried out, very much alive, on the shoulders of his admirers.

Stan described the *haus* to me. It was about 200 feet long and 50 feet high with superbly carved posts, covered with enemy blood. On display were drums, masks and weapons used in the fighting days, plus the heads of the enemies. Headhunting was the favoured sport of the day and the skin was pulled off by the teeth of the victors. Bloodied posts and heads would definitely have sent me over the edge!

I settled into this strange life reasonably well. I cooked quite often, though I was careful not to offend the *kuki boi*. Sometimes I had a drama – like snakebite or getting lost when I went to the loo at night. I read a great deal, wrote letters and at night listened to Radio America, or the European workers arguing about the war. Sometimes they sang their patriotic songs accompanied by Stefan playing excruciatingly bad piano accordian.

It didn't seem important that there were no clothes lines and wet clothes were laid out on the grass to dry and that we didn't have fresh eggs or fresh milk, only powdered, and that the flour *always* had weavils in it.

We didn't have phones but we had the amazing 'bush telegraph' where news would rapidly travel from one village to another. No one ever knew how it worked, but it did.

There were no pharmacies in Papua New Guinea and very few *hausiks* (hospitals). If we fell seriously ill we were canoed to the nearest hospital and in due course, flown south to Australia usually more dead than alive.

We had *polisbois* who wore black *laplaps* with black berets and sandals. *Doktabois* wore cream *laplaps* with a small red cross on the front and white short-sleeved shirts and bare feet. The *kali gang bois* (gaol labourers) wore red *laplaps* with black arrows and the *hausbois* wore white with borders of various colours. The average worker wore shorts and sandals.

Pidgin English was such a sensible language. It became customary to call the kitchen *haus kuk. Kalabus* was the gaol. A prostitute was called *meri bilong ol* – everyone's woman. A refrigerator was *bokis ais*. Many a shivering naked chook was found in the *bokis ais* awaiting the stew pot. The Bible was called *sampela pas belong nu testamen*; *mi praid* – afraid. *Kamap long hap ples yumi* was an invitation to come and visit and the answer: *Me laik kum long haus belong yu.*

The day the coconuts were collected was always a happy day for me because the starving kanaka dogs would be fed. The *boi* with a knife or *sarap* in his hand wrapped a circular strap around his ankles and then grabbed the tree forming a semi-circle with his feet. And up he would go. Confidently balancing he cut off coconuts and then down he slid. Once returned to the earth, he made a V-shape cut in the coconut from where we could drink and then threw the nuts to the dogs.

Stan decided he would not personally work out the tenders for any more Sepik work at this time. He planned to employ a qualified Indian engineer whom he felt had the expertise to deal with this wild terrain. He would leave the camp prepared and we would return to Port Moresby, finalise the plans with David the Indian and then move to our headquarters at Popondetta. This was a shrewd move and our new Indian colleague ultimately proved to be the right choice. It meant we had two big contracts going simultaneously; one based on the Sepik and the other in Popondetta. In the meantime Stan concentrated on repairing many of the wrecked roads and bridges in preparation for the first major bridge he was going to build.

After a couple of months, some of us returned to Port Moresby for a break before transferring to Popondetta. We had the tortuous journey back, this time with gusty winds and turbulent water with floating debris making the trip even more challenging than before. Our boat propellor blades jammed and we literally had to cut our way out through a narrow channel with a sort of pronged fork. The mosquitoes nearly drove me insane and even poor Bekky started to look a bit wan and fortunately lost interest in the crocodiles.

And then it rained, violently pelting down on us. Drenched and utterly miserable I remember feeling as though I had reached the end of the world. Some of the Sepik's strange mystical rites kept popping into my mind as we scooped out the water from the ever-filling boat, and I was genuinely frightened. I remember feeling hysterically grateful that we hadn't used the local canoes. They sat about one inch above the waterline and had a flat area at the back for cooking so those on board didn't need to stop to cook a meal if there were enemy tribes lurking. The natives handled these canoes skilfully but I knew it wasn't my sort of kitchen. We finally arrived back but I was a total write-off for weeks. It had been terrifying and yet we survived again.

Fortunately I had the privilege of meeting two charming Australian Irish brothers and their stories helped me forget some of the dangerous times in my trip. They had been gold prospectors for many years, found gold and were now millionaires and respectable. However the tales they told of their wild adventures beat any Errol Flynn film. They wanted to meet Stan who like them, was becoming a legend. They told me I was brave and who was I to contradict them? Momentarily I felt 10 feet tall.

The stories of how these two men survived in the jungle had me aching with laughter. For example, in a most delightful Irish manner, Danny explained that as the male genitals were the favourite nibbles with some tribes, 'I had to be assertive darlin' as they weren't getting my Irish dickie for an hors d'oeuvre'. I was told that he and his brother were not averse to bedding native girls and sometimes a marriage would be arranged and the blushing bride would be fiercely protective of her new toy. They were amazing gutsy men and they were feared and respected by blacks and whites from the Sepik to the Fly Rivers. I cheekily asked whether I could arrange a lunch for them at the District Commissioner's office and they both laughed and said their diaries were full!

Stan had an exciting letter from his family in Poland. They had all been meticulous, not corresponding directly over those post-war years for fear of Russian retaliation. However the family had survived well, one brother was an executive in the Department of Trade and another busy restructuring what was left of the family businesses. His two sisters taught the violin at the Conservatorium of Music and his young nephew David planned to become an orchestral conductor (he eventually conducted the Polish Symphony Orchestra). Mieszko, another nephew whose family had been in the Underground in Sweden, was a brilliant mathematician and eventually headed a large computer conglomerate in Stockholm.

As usual, my darling made a decision and then told me about it. He was going home to see his family. I had to wait in Moresby as he wasn't sure how it would be in Poland but if I wanted I could go to Europe later. I don't remember feeling pleased about this, but I couldn't begrudge him visiting his family. So off he went and once again I had to hope all would be well. I need not have been concerned. The family house and land was still intact and he held the title deeds. To celebrate the reunion he bought each family member a Fiat direct from the factory and down the road they came all in a row. It was a kind thought and millionaire Stanislau was the family's pride and joy even though no one could drive or afford petrol. Everywhere he went people in government cars tailed him.

Stan had no wish to live in Warsaw but he returned full of joy at seeing his family. He was impressed with the rebuilding of the city, exactly as it had been before the war, even using the original bricks.

He was happy to be back, thank goodness. His business was booming, he was employing Polish workmen who were not returning to Poland for various reasons, and he quite often remembered he loved me! He brought me back a large diamond ring, just what a girl needs in the New Guinea jungle, and a charming necklace of Polish amber 'for being a good girl'.

I had become firm friends with Catherine, a native woman whose husband Peter had been awarded a special medal for his bravery during the war. They had an intelligent and lively daughter called Debra. Stan generously arranged to help the family and ensured that Debra had the best education.

Life was improving for other indigenous people, although it was slow progress. Good education, decent housing and well-paid administration positions became more accessible. Some kids were sent south on scholarships (initially because they excelled in theology) but many were now starting extensive university courses in Queensland. As Australians we felt proud to have contributed so much towards these changes. It was a good time and as the country opened up, even more benefits came to the local people. The natives were taught trades and coffee, copra, cocoa and peanuts were exported. Australians were making good money too so it was worthwhile staying there. Stan certainly made money, but he worked so hard for it, very often from five in the morning until 10 at night.

There was so much to see and learn. I fell in love with the beauty of New Guinea, and that love remains with me today. I still remember the exhilaration I felt at the immensity of the scenery; the contrasts, the stillness of the black evening skies and bluest of day skies; the sometimes-eerie babbling, gabbling chorus of night birds calling to each other. I will always visualize the exquisite glory of pink sunsets and purple hills.

The dazzling emerald, mossgreen, scarlet, blue, maroon and yellow hues of that most divine of birds, the bird of paradise, still fills my heart with wonder. I have seen 14 species with their coloured sparkling discs, and the exquisite feathers that looked like coloured flags on wires.

The diverse beauty of New Guinea was breathtaking. Perched alongside magnificent rivers in steep ravines were tidy villages with their round thatch-roofed houses looking as though they were toppling down the mountainsides, trying to catch up with the self-sown gardens.

How different the tribes were in dress, hairstyles and features. Some had frizzy hair, some tassels, others wore elaborate wigs like great big hats or cockatoo headdresses or *cuscus* fur wound into a form of hairnet. Some decorated themselves with bean and bamboo stick necklaces, bodies were pig-greased in one village but covered with bird of paradise feathers in another. Tattooed faces were popular in some areas whilst other tribes featured crocodile-pattern markings. The older tribe members used vegetable paints to adorn the body, the younger ones commercial paint. But one thing they had in common – they looked so very old. The lack of protein in the diet and the hard life took its toll and they often looked 20 years older than they actually were.

Many things worried and distressed me, such as the incessant nose picking or what was worse; a thumb on one nostril and the blow out the other. There was the rancid smell of the pig kills (sometimes 1000 to 1500 in one day) for a special ceremony. And how incongruous to see the protective behaviour of the owners walking their piglets tied by one leg as we would walk the family dog or the *meris* with piglets on their breasts fattening them up for the moment of death.

I can still almost smell the unwashed bodies and the ghastly Muruk tobacco in the enervating heat. I wonder if the girls whose parents can't afford a bride price of $200 plus pigs, still 'lose face'.

Anyway, I was off again, to yet another adventure. I wondered what Popondetta would be like, especially as I would be living in a 'proper' house. I had become used to camps but to have my very own corner with my husband would be special. Wouldn't it? Because we intended moving to Popondetta for a long time, I had many goodbyes to say. Judith Brady came over from Lae as she and the family were making their first move overseas to a London posting and it was sad because we didn't know if we would meet again. But we had fun although I fell out of a car taking a bend, which wasn't too pleasant. I still have weals on my legs from the gravel.

12

Popondetta

Once again, I closed up my little *donga*, packed all my clothes, books and records and Bekky, Ras and I took off in a small plane for Popondetta. Bekky was a sociable dog and happy to be flying with humans again and not in a baggage compartment. After all she was a much-travelled pooch and liked wandering around chatting to the natives and showing off to Ras who was still in a cage. Someone had been eating crocodile, the odour of which remains in the skin, and this caused Bekky a little confusion. As she put her nose up to the Papuan's face and sniffed, he rolled his eyes and dribbled with fear.

As usual, I was nervous flying in a small plane. There were no safety aids and the pilot's attempts to find the gaps in the clouds without running out of fuel contributed to my discomfort and fear. When George the pilot asked, 'Do you know where we are at the moment?' he wasn't joking! We were so close to the mountains I felt I could put my hand out and stroke them. Fortunately, despite George, we had a smooth trip and arrived safe and sound in Popondetta. Charlie, Louis, Steve and Tom welcomed me and Stan's chief 'leading hand' studied me with a practised eye. Dear Narku was also there to greet me; his big smile of welcome remains a delightful memory.

The camp was adequate. There were thatch-roofed huts, a *kuk haus* and our little hut. The toilets (holes in the ground) and bucket showers were away from the camp and surrounded by hessian for privacy.

I put my books around the *kuk haus* to share but noticed my Simone de Beauvoir did not have the well-worn look that their 'Man' magazines sported.

Popondetta with its nearby active volcano, Mt Lamington, is nestled amongst the rain forest and oil palms of Oro Province which lies between the Owen Stanley Range and the Solomon Sea. In the fifties it was an attractive town with numerous, interesting towns close by; Tufi was spectacular, Wanigela had good reefs, and Yiaku village produced excellent tapa cloth. The prime agricultural land enriched by volcanic ash supported rubber, oil palm, cocoa, copra and cattle. The Queen Alexandra birdwing butterfly, the biggest butterfly in the world, was found only in Oro.

There were only two things to mar my joy. Finding the toilets at night and returning home was one. Somehow perched over a hole left me feeling vulnerable to whatever was crawling around or possibly slithering so I usually had a panicky return trip. The other problem was our bed. When I hear about 96 positions in sex, I can add a few of my own design. It was necessary if I intended to keep my limbs mobile. The beds were timber blocks and slats. I can tell you, after surviving that bed, I can sleep on anything to this day.

With the promise of my house being completed 'soon' I settled happily into a routine. Narku and I cooked for the 20 Europeans. We provided the *linebois* with the same food as we ate but they preferred to cook and eat separately, and then frequently join us after the meal for a song, game of darts or cards.

Even in the heat, roasts and curries, braised chops and stews were popular. I had special rooms to store the potatoes and bread, and we had to make a lot of damper, which always reminded me of stories about my dad as a young lad in the Australian bush. The first time I saw weavils in the flour I told Stan we would have to get some more and he just laughed and told me it was good protein.

You'd be surprised just how good mouldy potatoes can taste smartened up with chopped fried bacon and onions, and how tasty roast dinners can be made out of tinned mackerel if you're hungry enough. There was always plenty of bacon because I used to buy it in great rolls. We had a cooked breakfast and I learnt what to cook by the amount of rum bottles lined up in the morning – the boozier the night the fattier the breakfast. If they all had hangovers, greasy bacon and egg was the best or large bowls of bread-dunking soup. Soup was always on the wood stove and nothing was wasted – it all went in the pot. Alternatively there were cold cornish-style pasties if hangovers were *really* grim! Lunch was cold meat if we had leftover roast (often pork) or poultry if we could buy locally, or the *bois* could shoot something and we would make a type of stirfry. Salads were made with whatever we could get, often locally-grown native beans, ginger and garlic. Everything was heavily salted, and the men often ate handfuls of salt or salt tablets as well.

I clearly remember the time Narku handed me my first pig's head; he was so proud and I didn't have the heart to tell him I had no idea what to do with the damm thing. Fortunately, I had the old *Green and Gold* cookbook and sure enough there it was: 'How to cook a pig's head'. I can still see the whiskers floating on top and those accusing little eyes. I made brawn although not quite like Mother's. It was a bit wobbly with the heat but it was wolfed down accompanied by a great deal of dribbling down unshaved chins. This, combined with the smells of 20 unwashed guys with their shoes off who had never heard of deodorant, made an indelible impression on my nasal nerves. It was one of the nights

I sat outside alone playing Brahm's *First Symphony* and contemplating the blue-black sky and my sanity.

We respected each other until a fight started and there was often tension as we still had a League of Nations in the camp. There would be careless talk between those border Ukraines, Poles and Germans who never quite knew where they belonged and boom! These blokes didn't muck around. If knives and axes disappeared we panicked and had to be vigilant for days. I can remember one night a German from the township called to have a drink. Stan had always avoided him and I wondered why; then I saw an erased area on the German's arm that probably meant ex-SS! I thought Stan was going to kill him. He left running and he wasn't the only one shaking with fear.

But then on a peaceful tropical evening I would melt as Stefan played his accordian, and Mick who had joined our team his guitar, and they would sing haunting songs of their countries. I'd ask them to explain songs because most sounded so sad. They usually told about the loss of loved ones, or homes, or prison, or countries. Sometimes the song was about a young girl who suicided because her loved one was killed during the war. Once they asked me to sing an Australian song, and I only knew one, *Waltzing Matilda*, and I didn't know all the words. I felt embarrassed.

Eventually I graduated to picking up the fuel; we had different fuel storage areas and Narku and I would take a big diesel truck and collect whatever was required. These were long trips through the jungle but I enjoyed the change. I had my first bad trip. I had to cross the river and I couldn't understand why they were trying to wave me back. On arrival I saw, to my horror, a *meri* had just lost her legs to a crocodile. It was just frightful; I can still see the poor dying girl. I don't remember how I got through that day and I didn't get the hug from Stan that I needed. I was required to cope.

I believe I am an environmental nut, but I have never been able to feel anything but horror for 'crocagators' as my daughter used to call them. Author Robert Ruarks's description of an alligator's lair with a live human propped up for a future meal, haunted my dreams for weeks. Robert who came to stay with us in the jungle whilst writing his book, *Inside New Guinea*, was a charming man and excellent company. Stan took him on trips into the jungle and in due course his book was deservedly an outstanding success.

Our house was nearly finished in Popondetta Township and I looked forward to becoming 'civilised'. It was only a little timber box of a house but it was just for us. I had shelving put in to hold my beloved books and records that fortunately hadn't gathered mould, and I intended putting up the inevitable curtains. I think I had a psychological problem regarding curtains, but don't ask me what. Maybe I felt insecure!

There were quite a few people scattered around the Popondetta area and once we moved into our little house we were welcomed warmly and we lived an almost normal existence for a while. Our new neighbours were mainly plantation people working very hard for very little and always, with independence looming, there was the worry of whether the new government of Australia would keep its promise and provide reimbursement. Stan was a generous host and once the residents had become used to his accent and his sparse grammar we spent many happy hours with them.

In due time as the crew worked further afield, the men didn't return for lunch and Narku would arrange something for them to take. I would often pack a tomato and bread and a tin of sardines that Stan enjoyed even in the heat, and take this to him. We sat with the butterflies and orchids overlooking his road or bridge feeling fortunate to have these close moments.

Considering the New Guinea terrain it was impressive how Stan's roads and bridges usually survived the frequent rains and landslides. They were rough by today's standards but I doubt if any contractor could have done better at that time. They laid the foundations for the future.

There were tenders out for projects in Goroka and Wau, and I was keeping my fingers crossed we would win some and we could revisit old friends in these towns and also Lae. Stan was once again successful. He was driving the opposition construction firms wild and there was a lot of 'dirty pool' played at times by others. This really got up Stan's nose, as he was a totally honest man. He won the tender linking Goroka to Lae and ultimately Arabica coffee became a good cash crop for Goroka and Kainantu.

I was looking forward to a few days in Wau; at 1300m altitude we could be assured of chilly nights and the change from constant humidity was like a tonic. There was still a little gold trading going on even though the gold had petered out by the start of World War II, and I planned to call at one of the fossiker's houses bearing a sign: '*Salim gol long hae*' (gold sold here). Stan was interested in the dangerous Watut River but I wanted to bargain at the markets for carvings and pots for my new house.

I must have picked up a little surprise on this trip, because during the night I woke up feeling something on my face. It was a hairy mother spider with a body the size of a small plate. I screamed and hit it off my face only to discover I was wearing dozens (although it felt like thousands) of premmy spider babies, left on me after her hasty departure. I was assured I had 'brought it with me' and I was too stupefied to argue.

Another day I won't forget I spent picking unidentified bugs off the growing coffee. The removal of these coffeeplant-eating bugs became a community concern and it was heart warming to watch everyone helping everyone else hand pick these bugs. Because we were there we helped too. We threw the bugs into hessian bags and they were burnt, the only known way at that time to get rid of them.

We returned to Popondetta and because everything was going so well, Stan worked on his new tender and then one night said, 'We go to Mummy for a month and meet the Germans' (my aunt's family). With a degree of trepidation I agreed – I wasn't at all sure how things would go in little old Adelaide. I mentioned to Stan that we had no suitable clothes for the southern climate so he grunted, 'We go Sydney and buy plunty. You gut millions now – go, enjoy'.

Having settled down happily in my new home in Popondetta, Stan now decided I should return to Moresby after our holiday. He knew the contract would take three years, and he felt I could fill my days more constructively in Port Moresby than in Popondetta. This was quite true, but oh, he was difficult! David had said he would always have me back in District Office even if only for a short time, so that's what Stan planned. And as a mere wife who was I to argue?

13

Australian holiday

With a smile on my face, a bulging wallet and a loving husband, I boarded the DC10 for Sydney. My Bekky and Ras were not too happy having to stay behind with friends even though I assured them it was a well-earned holiday.

We arrived at Ushers Hotel in Sydney known as the 'New Guinea Water Hole.' Stan left to buy something to wear, and I went off to have a facial and hairdo at Elizabeth Arden Salon followed by shopping. The crowds were actually scary and the traffic worse than I recalled but I felt the facial doing me good. The shopping was superb and I remember the absolute joy when I realised I had spent 7000 pounds in one day just on me and I could do the same again every day if I wanted to.

I discarded the pink-and-white-spotted frock, cardigan and cheap white sandals for an elegant navy suit, fine silk stockings and girdle, a zany hat and gorgeous suede-and-crocodile-trimmed shoes and matching handbag. I felt good about that crocodile. All new cosmetics and a hairdo finished me off very nicely thank you.

Stan and I agreed to meet in the foyer at Ushers for drinks with old friends at 6 pm but Stan passed me four times without recognising me! I could say it was just because I was wearing a hat. Eventually, when I saw him growing a little rosy-pink I coughed politely. He turned around and looked at me with downright adoration – I had passed muster! He too looked gorgeous may I say. We settled down to total decadence; flaming Alexanders, French champagne, expensive restaurants, great clothes, wonderful beds. And we were in love, with not a worry in the world. We couldn't take our eyes or hands off each other. A far cry from canoeing on the Sepik!

Eventually we took a flight to Adelaide and of course Mother was ecstatic. A grand dinner party of welcome was arranged at Hal and Gladdis and Stan was actually nervous. It was quite funny because all the men of the family were still Freemasons, anti-Catholic and against 'Balts' (people born in certain European areas). Stan really had his work cut out to get them on side. Typically he wooed the women first. Then it was easy and by the end of the evening, everyone was 'eating out of his hand'.

The table was magnificent, the German girls had excelled, and everyone was dressed up and did us proud. Of course there was soup, as I had told them he was a soup person. But the soup was pea soup because it was wintry weather and Stan had a second helping because it was delicious. The result was disaster – *wind*! He was up and down every five minutes and no one knew why. He was becoming more and more agitated and embarrassed and in the end when he had been missing for some time I went and found him in the toilet. Of course he confessed the problem and I decided to make light of it to the family and nicknamed him 'Poopypants'. We all finally had a good laugh; he was a great success.

We travelled to Kangaroo Island to Gladdi and Hal's cottage on the cliffs of Vyvonne Bay and lazed, fished, ate and drank, and Stan decided our whiting was the best fish in the world.

It was a happy time; everyone liked each other and we saw quite a bit of South Australia, which was green and lush at that time of the year. Stan bought Mother a new car although she didn't drive. He said, 'So she learn to drive,' and organised her lessons.

We had a few 'happenings' as I like to call them. A nosy woman called Shirley was determined to meet Stan, so she and her husband called uninvited to Mother's house. She talked on and on pretentiously culminating in fashion chat regarding broderie anglaise.

I sensed from Stan's expression something was looming as he turned to Shirley's husband and said, 'Man you might like listening to rubbish talk at home, so you take your woman home now,' and showed them the door. Oh dear!

Another night we had been nipping at the Scotch. Stan's voice was enormous at any time and a timid English neighbour toddled over the road, popped her head around our patio and nervously whispered, 'Is everything alright here?'

14

Mieszco

Stan's Polish nephew who lived in Sweden had wanted to visit Australia and when he learnt we were going to Adelaide he decided this was the time to meet. He really was the 'unknown quantity'. Stan had not met him but he had a reputation as a brilliant scientist and mathematician in Sweden. Something to do with a new thing called computers. He was to stay with us but wanted to visit our great opal-mining town Coober Pedy.

Visit he did but we lost contact with him once he was in Coober Pedy. However he was a big boy now, married with a child, so we weren't unduly worried. Well we should have been. We had Interpol ringing, MI5, the Swedish Consulate and Swedish Police. Did we know where he was?

No one could find him and a search commenced – all the mining holes were to be checked and there were thousands of them. Fortunately he was discovered having the time of his life with a miner from Finland, living underground and drinking lots of vodka. Stan was very angry.

Mieszco returned to us, Interpol was contacted, his wife and child were reassured he was still alive, and for a day or two he behaved. Then he misbehaved at a party which was the last straw.

Stan said, 'I kick his Swedish arse' and put him on a plane for Sweden. On Mieszco's return, Stan bought him a 200-acre farm out of Stockholm.

15

Back to New Guinea

It was a good holiday despite these upsets and we returned to
New Guinea rejuvenated by the break. I stayed in Moresby as
Stan wanted to visit each camp and thoroughly check things out
and Ras and tail-wagging Bekky were flown back. An English-
woman who had taken over my job, took the opportunity on my
return to holiday with her family in England, so I started work
again immediately. When I took a few days leave without pay to
join Stan somewhere we arranged temps.

David Marsh handed me the keys to the Security Files, so
with the myriad of other duties we handled the Courts, Land
Titles, Security, District Office and the Patrol Officers as well as
media liaison. Professionally it was a busy and fulfilling period
for me and I revelled in it. My newfound maturity did not go
unnoticed and I was happy to take more responsibility as it was
offered. Every day was a challenge but we were a team of dedicated, some might say obsessed people who loved the New Guinea
people and country, and we delighted at seeing our planning and
work come to fruition. We worked long hours for moderate wages
but our main challenge was the race against time.

It was 1958 and Moresby was changing. There was far more camaraderie between the blacks and the whites. The administration
was providing good homes for both the indigenous employees
and the Australians, based on level of employment rather than
race. There was an improvement in the dressing and general
grooming of the native people. Many Australians were returning
south on completion of their contracts, making room for the educated Papuans and private enterprise was developing rapidly
amongst many of the educated indigenous people. Although the
standard of living in the large towns was improving, the villages
were still relying on the sale of their magnificent crafts and produce
and their lifestyles had not changed significantly.

We had created an efficient public service with, importantly,
mutual respect. Inflation was low and productivity high. Education
services were being expanded and wages were gradually approaching parity.

The pressure was really on now for Australian private enterprise
in Papua New Guinea to finalise as many contracts as possible
knowing that handover to the local people was approaching. We
were hearing rumbles from the south about a Labour Party politi-
cian called Gough Whitlam who was pushing for independence.
We all knew that to give New Guinea independence too soon
would be disastrous for the people but we were risking United
Nations contempt as 'colonialists' if we didn't. So it looked as
though New Guinea was going to be pushed and shoved into
independence regardless of what was good for them. We felt we
needed 10 more years at the very least but this now seemed
unlikely. Even though intertribal wars were no longer a common
occurrence the leaders still feared they could lose power to old
enemies. This lack of trust between tribes made advancement all
the more challenging. There were over 800 languages, with some
spoken by only a few hundred people, and there was concern that

Papua could be swallowed by the wealthier New Guinea. To further complicate the situation, the island was divided up with the west under Dutch control (transferring to Indonesia in 1963) and Australia governing the north and south. The situation was complex and so were our obligations to our New Guinea friends. Black and white were equally afraid of letting go too soon.

Stan was talking of buying his own plane, which he thought would make travel easier. I spoke sharply and he, for once, diplomatically dropped the idea. Captain Stanley I could do without.

Now based in Port Moresby again, I needed accommodation. I stayed with Peg and John Rutherford for a few days before deciding on a rental house. There were some interesting new homes overlooking the coast and I decided to lease an attractively furnished home with a view.

It all seemed so strange initially, living in a civilised atmosphere of tiled bathrooms and toilets, even en suites and I must say going to the loo was a joy. We still had a driveable Peugeot in Moresby and I was reasonably content with the company of good friends but I missed Stan, and strangely enough I missed the bush – it had a hold on me.

It was good to see Maeva and Frank Mollinger again. I will never forget their generosity in the early years when we had nothing. They had three children and another on the way and we would pop in to say hello. We would open a couple of wines and they always insisted we share a meal. Frank was a handsome Dutch West New Guinean and Maeva was part French. They were excellent company and made the most wonderful meals from their homegrown vegetables and freshly-caught fish. The little they had they shared with everyone. They were a much loved and respected couple.

And to catch up with delightful Margaret Johns who had been

such a friend not just to me but to so many. What an intelligent gutsy lady she was. She was going south and she would be sadly missed. Not so her millionaire husband, hated by everyone. But that's another story. I will give you a hint though – it took her 10 years to fight him in court and although she had no money and no legal support she won.

It was good to have a picture theatre and I was so enthusiastic that I took a part-time job a couple of nights a week in the box office. It filled in some lonely hours and I could see all the shows after being film starved for years. The bloke who managed the theatre didn't know me at all but I began to suspect he was a small time crook. I was talking to Inspector Mike Thomas one day and I mentioned discrepancies I noticed between takings at the pictures and the figures given to the owners, but I couldn't work out how it was being done. Mike arranged to call in one night and put on a bit of an act for all to see and sure enough the manager had been breaking the ticket rolls, taping them back together and pocketing the difference. It had been quite a profitable business for him over the years.

I started making new friends such as Lorraine, a model from Sydney who was living with a devilishly attractive Czech called Andre who was, unfortunately, penniless. When Stan flew over for a weekend we celebrated their engagement at a village called Iduabada. What a disaster! I was sitting on Andre's lap in a joking way, talking to Lorraine and looking at her engagement ring. All of a sudden there was mayhem. I was picked up and thrown through two doors, landing on a cement path. On top of me came a table, two chairs and a radio. And there was Stanley-boy, red faced with fury, heaving poor Andre by the neck to throw him on top of me.

This was no happy hubby. And guess who else was not smiling? Me! By now, to make matters worse, the Iduabadans had come out to see who was winning and as I jumped up and rushed inside, they cheered me as a *namba wan sinubada* (Motu for misis). In my life I had not felt such anger.

Stan muttered, 'Get in car – we go,' but I just ignored him, which left me feeling I could be breathing my last breath in this world. He gave me a malevolent look as he walked out and I heard the car go.

The party was ruined and everyone was stunned and afraid for me. Futilely I tried to rally everyone into a happy mood, but I was mortified. I was eventually driven home and fortunately nothing was said when I arrived there and made my way to sleep in the spare room. Nothing was discussed, no apologies were forthcoming, and I was absolutely frigid. The Polish mates were brought home for dinner and I went out and came home late and the atmosphere just got worse. And then the ice was broken. Stan often clicked his fingers at me and pointed when he wanted an ashtray, just a wee bit chauvinistic of course, but a habit I usually tolerated. He did this in front of the Poles when I arrived home late one night.

I put my hands on my hips and said, 'Are you paralysed?'

You could have heard a pin drop. And then he smiled. And I was so surprised, I smiled back. Hopefully, it was the start of a new era – if I lived that long!

I became a rugby addict. Our local Port Moresby team played the Chinese and the whites and it was a fast and dirty game. The major Papuan player was a handsome bloke called John Kuputin (now Sir John Kaputin) and he was a hero to us all, particularly a pretty Australian teacher. They were lovers and wanted to marry. As this was the first marriage between an Australian woman and Papuan man things had to be done correctly so she went south and made application to, I think, Mr Hasluck, Federal Minister for Territories. It is pleasing to report that when I last heard, the marriage was still working well. I don't know whether Kaputin took other wives.

Moresby was on a roll. Rich oil deposits had been discovered. It was decided to cap the holes and not encourage overseas investment until independence had been achieved. Decisions about the oil fields would then be up to the New Guineans.

By 1959, I was busy at work and not seeing much of Stan at all. I decided I had better join him in Goroka for a while or I wouldn't have a marriage, so once again David gave me leave without pay and I returned to a bush camp, in this case a particularly rough one, as they were being constantly moved and reassembled. Stan was working long hours every day now and everyone was exhausted and my darling Bekky missed the civilised house in Moresby with the overhead fans and the couch to sleep on.

Even though I was lonely at times and conditions were harsh, my short trip to Goroka was a delightful, well-earned break and a chance to spend a brief time with Stan. Goroka was beautiful with its green sun-kissed valley surrounded by majestic purple-blue hills. It seemed that time stood still there.

The native people were charming and splendidly dressed and the Bena Bena girls were stunning with their exquisite lace-like beaded collars of all sizes and colours. Stan was glad we were together and told me we would be visiting Mt Hagen and Madang.

Mt Hagen was a tranquil, friendly town with the main road running along one side of an airstrip lined with casuarinas, poinsettia and hibiscus. There were sawmills and a couple of shops, a small hospital and school and many missions, and hansenide (leper) colonies. It's hard to believe that by 1972, hatred towards the whites had reached a point where a European man would be stoned in this main street at lunchtime and European women raped.

The local Mt Hagen people were said to most closely resemble those from the Stone Age civilization. They wore hair tassles hanging from the top of their heads and added the most extraordinary adornments to their hair, such as leaves and cigarette package labels. The women and children saved all their clipped curls and added animal fur, and the overall result looked surprisingly Afro-American.

Some of their dressing was similar to the Masai of Kenya. They wore wrap-around garments in vivid colours and the most incredible belts made of foot-wide carved bands of wood bark (I never did find out how these were put on) and loin cloths in the front and 'ass grass' over their rear ends.

Even though the district looked fairly desolate, it was producing coffee and tea, and cattle were proving profitable. Passionfruit was bought by Cottees for their popular drinks and pyrethrum, a daisy plant used in insecticides, was successfully grown but was harder to cultivate.

We enjoyed a short flight over the mountains and the great Ramu River to beautiful Madang and we started to perspire at just the thought of the aircraft doors opening. By the time we had jeeped the eight miles from the airstrip to the town, our clothes were wet through.

We were staying with hospitable business friends of Stan's, and after cold beers and a shower we took off driving along the water's edge to Kalibobo Point, a memorial built to the wartime coast watchers.

Stan was absolutely fascinated by Madang. We drove through a teak forest the Germans had planted during World War I, saw old Junkers planes from World War II and walked over an old bomber airstrip. But the best was yet to come; bridges that had been built during the war. While Stan looked at those, my eyes were rivetted on the streams underneath infested with huge, ravenous *pukpuks*. I think I had become obsessional about crocodiles.

There were interesting stories of the war years and we

POW to bridge builder

A former member of the Polish underground during the Second World War is now a successful building contractor in the Northern District.

He is Mr Stan Rybarz who came to the Territory in 1950.

His latest building project is putting a 410 ft. bridge across the Kumusi River to provide a road link between Popondetta and Kokoda.

TRICKY

At present, to get from one town to the other you have to ford the Kumusi, which can be trick when it is in flood.

Mr Ryzarz said he was imprisoned by the Germans while working in the u n d e r-ground.

After travelling and working in Italy and Britain he joined the Merchant Navy and made his way to Australia.

He went to Rabaul when he arrived in the Territory where he worked on Administration housing projects.

He later worked as foremane for a private construction firm and finally went into business for himself.

H i s construction firm has had many jobs around Popondetta under contract from the Administration.

Mr Rybarz has a European foreman on his latest job and two other European staff, and apart from this uses local labor.

He says he is very satisfied with their hard and consientious work.

wondered how the Japanese survived the dysentery and malaria. They were known to have walked to the mouth of the Ramu River and then crossed it by barge then travelled up the Sepik to Marienberg towards Wewak. This was a notoriously unhealthy area in those days – cerebral malaria was rife and deadly and there was no cure for it at that time.

We returned to the little township and Stan went off to talk boring men's business and I walked around the little town streets still shaded by the huge rain trees the Germans had planted. Madang was the New Guinea Shangri-la.

Returning to the camp, I realised how glad Stan was to be with me for a short time but didn't want the complications of a wife for too long. He suggested I go overseas for a holiday, and we would work the timing out as best we could so he could join me in Paris. It sounded great, but I didn't believe him. At least he was more relaxed and we had a happy time, making love on the worst bed I ever knew and eating the worst food in the toughest country. With a promise he would get over to Moresby as soon as possible, which again I didn't believe, Bekky and I returned to civilisation.

I decided that when I did holiday again Bekky should go home to my mother. I couldn't face leaving her with strangers again; she deserved a good retirement and Mum adored her.

Well, that was the plan – then dreadful news! A bush phone call to District Office: Stan had been in a bad accident, one of the earthmovers had tipped over with him in it. He had been rushed to hospital and was in a critical condition.

I grabbed a small bag and Bek and I took off again on the first plane. Stan looked so bad I wondered if he was going to survive. He managed a wan smile and the long wait started.

He had suffered a stroke as well as many bad injuries from the fall and as the weeks went on, his impatience became a major problem as his arm and hand just wouldn't function properly. It really was a harrowing time. Eventually he was given a ball to squeeze and the language was an education to all staff. In fact initially, everyone was terrified of him. One female doctor used to literally shake when seeing Stan, though Stan assured me it was passion not fear!

Each day a battle would be on – would Stan do his hand exercises? He would roar about 'f#%*! stupid broads who had him playing f#%*! stupid games with f#%*! stupid balls' and assured them when he could walk again he would show them 'balls'. It was difficult to remember how serious everything was because he was so funny. The ward had a roster system and when caring for Stan, each nurse would twitter with the conflicting emotions of fear, excitement, horror and always anticipation, of what I am not sure! And, as if that wasn't enough, he had a leg in plaster that he swore he was going to remove. We presumed he meant the plaster not the leg but one couldn't be sure of anything, and we apprehensively watched each day wondering what further joy he was going to deliver to us tortured souls.

Stan was worrying about penalty rates; each non-working day was costing a fortune and without a qualified engineer on this job everything had stopped.

I moved to the camp full of bored men with idle hands and booze in the hope this would keep the peace. Also, due to the accident, there was costly damage to the equipment.

With the help of Charlie and Frank, I managed to make a list of requirements and approximate costs. The boys assured me they could get the equipment going again. I, probably too smugly I think, told Stan things were going well and our plans for the camp. Well that was my first mistake.

The Polak was very quiet for a while and we all thought he had settled down and was trying hard to be a good boy – that was the second mistake! He did his walking around the hospital, and his hand and arm exercises. He always seemed to be busily drawing and writing, until one day he erupted. Bedclothes were thrown around, the cast was cut off, and with one leg bigger than the other a red-faced apparition wheelchaired into the camp. Stan had secretly organised transport with one of his *linebois* and had escaped the hospital.

This remarkable husband of mine then sat in his chair, issuing orders as usual, and had a pulley erected to the equipment. He then learnt how to pull himself up and with a boy to assist with the levers he couldn't manage, he drove the machinery to complete the contract. I might add he beat the contract time even though half-paralysed.

I had a long talk with the doctor about the implication of Stan's actions in regard to his future health, and he just shrugged his shoulders and said he liked Stan's chances of survival better than his staff's if Stan returned to the hospital!

He stressed that Stan would have to be checked regularly, that he had to take certain medication and that it was up to me to see this occurred. I said that I noticed he had omitted to tell me how and he smiled wryly and said if one was desperate enough one would find a way, and being female should help.

Stan was out with the crew working a full day and I was totally superfluous, except at bedtime! However I had to try and get the message through that he was living dangerously.

I decided that seeing him turn purple was probably unavoidable so I tapped on the table at dinner one night and told everyone that I would be returning to Moresby *but* that I had something else to say. And I then told my audience what the doctor had said and that Stan could not be trusted. They all laughed but I made them promise they would ensure that Stan obeyed the medical orders. Stan was not amused and later, in private, he started to rebuke me. I verbally let him 'have it!' He took it like a lamb and I think he begrudgingly enjoyed my concern. I knew that the blokes would make sure he carried out doctor's orders so I said goodbye, confident he would be okay. I felt drained – he really could be trying to say the least!

I returned to my lonely life of work and trying to fill in the hours. I started looking after the Kirke children when Craig, our local solicitor and his wife Pam had social commitments. They treated me warmly and I liked being in a family environment again. I started half-heartedly planning an overseas trip, trying to incorporate Stan's ridiculous itinerary, which just made me feel lethargic. My heart wasn't really in it – to go on my own wasn't exciting.

And then an almost unbelievable but delightful bombshell: the joy of pregnancy. Stan's sperm count was low due to the privations during the war years. I'm sure you would all like to know how I conned him into finding out about his problem without letting him know he had a problem. It would leave you breathless! Anyway, my chances of falling pregnant were poor, so this indeed seemed a miracle. I think I shared my news with the whole world, and Stan was proud and pleased.

Dear David let me stay on working manageable hours and it was a wonderful time for me, carrying my baby. In due course, I was booked into Taurama Hospital with all the modern conveniences! It was a long tin shed with arc-mesh walls – just like my first house in Lae. They did have a toilet block but it was always flooding and patients had to wade in amongst all sorts of little surprises floating around the toilet floors.

The maternity ward had twenty beds along each arc-mesh wall, with an occasional piece of galvanised iron for good luck. Mother came up for the birth, nearly fainted when she saw the hospital, and learnt that we had to 'go it alone'as the native women did, without any anaesthetic. The great moment arrived. I was the only white in the 40-bed ward and the *meris* warmly welcomed me. They were so dignified – they would quietly go into the labour ward and in a short while have their little babies and come back tired and smiling. Not me! I was the last one in, spent the longest time in and was certainly the noisiest. I moaned and yowled; I was a disgrace! The nurse chuckled when she saw the book I mistakenly believed I could read between labour pains. I had asked her what it was going to be like and she said, 'It's rather like bad constipation'.

The day after my beautiful daughter Jane was born, Cathie, another white, arrived to also deliver a first baby. I passed on the nurse's information to her very smugly. We all heard Cathie leaving the labour ward many hours later yelling: 'Where is that Rybarz woman – I'm going to kill her!' She repeated her plan after an instrument birth when she saw her baby for the first time looking a bit funny, elongated is a good word, and told them to send it back.

That night, sleeping fitfully from exhaustion, I felt something around my tender front end, then searing pain, suffocation and stark fear. In the blackness of night a wiry intruder or intruders greased all over with foul-smelling pig fat had removed my bloody towelling and were forcing some giant thing up raw bleeding areas that had just been through child birth. I was being raped. It felt like I was being cut to pieces and it was never going to end. What a dreadful, sickening experience. I felt defiled and dishonoured which was much worse than the pain. I will never forget the horror and I relive it when I hear the word rape. I tried to push him or them away but I had no strength. I still don't know if it was one person or many persons, white or coloured. I couldn't grab skin because of the pig fat, so I gripped hair and tried to throw my attacker off. I tend to think it was more than one because I seemed to be struck around the head and face during the rape and while I tried to cope with that, damp earth and gravel were shoved into my mouth to stop me screaming. I thought I was going to choke.

After what seemed hours of this violent, loathsome attack a quiet, relaxed nurse carrying a tray of pills and a torch toddled in, took one look, threw the tray in the air dropping pills everywhere and bolted screaming. If it hadn't been so bloody serious, it would have been funny. The rapists ran, I hoped with head pains and near baldness. But I was in a bad way. Rape is always vile but 24 hours after my baby girl was born was abominable, loathsome hell! I can remember gabbling and crying and shaking uncontrollably. There was blood everywhere and I was covered in it and I felt fury at the violation and shamed. People with torches and lamps were running around vigorously but without plan and there was an acerbic quality in the ward. I must have been given some medication about this time because fortunately I don't remember much from then until next day.

I do remember Inspector Mike Thomas interviewing me, I don't remember when. I had a succession of white and black men with bad reputations paraded in front of me for days. I nearly lost my milk and the joy of my daughter's birth was temporarily tarnished. But the investigation proved interesting.

The conclusion was reached that a male person/s had been watching me for many years, goodness knows why. The Police went back to the old *donga* and found 16 peepholes – I had been watched from every angle, in the shower, the bedroom, the kitchen.

A track had been cut from the main road through the lush vegetation for easy, private access to the *donga*. So I had been a source of reliable entertainment for a long time. I could feel my confidence disappearing. I was terrified by this invasion of privacy, and I knew my days of feeling secure had probably gone forever. Also I had to face the disgrace of rape.

The story made headlines in the paper, although Inspector Mike wouldn't allow details, and Stanley-dear arrived roaring like a bull, threatening to sue everyone. It was dreadful but at least as a result of my attack, doors were placed on the hospital wards! We never did find out who raped me. I was scared of everything, particularly men, and jumped when anyone came near me. What helped me get through it all was the love that Stan and I felt for our beautiful daughter.

My life started to take on a veneer of normality. Ironically I ended up with so much milk, I fed premmie babies. I hated the indignity of the milking machines but when I heard of the cannisters of my frozen breast milk being flown or sent by boat up river to other mothers, I felt very proud to be helping.

I was encouraged to move back to the old *donga* (which was now electrically shock-wired on the roof and safely enclosed) with Mother, Jane and Bekky and I started to relax a little with people around me. The isolation of the other house had fed my nervousness. Mother stayed for a while but when she returned south I unfortunately lost confidence again.

Another tragedy occurred. This was an accident to a dear friend who was married to a hard-working Ukranian lad but had taken a second job waitressing to build up the bank balance needed for their new home. She was wearing a synthetic frock that ignited while she was pumping the kerosene stove in the restaurant and she was burnt alive. By the time I had handled the funeral and her distraught parents I was fit for nothing.

My wonderful daughter was cooped up with me in a virtual prison. I had good supportive friends but it wasn't enough and I felt I was letting Jane down. When Stan flew home for his next visit he was shocked at my pale thin appearance and my anxious demeanour. We discussed my fears and we both knew I would have to return to Adelaide for a while. I felt a failure and emotionally unstable. Sadly I packed up the few things I wanted to keep, including my jazz records, and gave my Papuan friend Margaret everything else. Stan would take Bekky with him until I could make decisions about the future. To take her south meant six months quarantine and I just couldn't face that. It was a wrench for me but I knew she and Stan were good mates and she knew all the crew and would be loved and looked after.

The indigenous people were flocking over the border from West New Guinea as the time for Indonesian control approached. They were full of shocking stories about their treatment. We were also hearing frightening reports about East Timor and realised that it was only a matter of time before there would be massive upheavals in that area. Added to this, Bougainville was getting very jumpy about the mining that was going on and wanted to separate from the Solomon Islands.

All these stories were unsettling for both blacks and whites, and the good camaraderie that had built up between us was strained. I was now terrified of everything and everyone. There was no choice for me at this time: I had to leave and it broke my heart.

We trundled down to the old DC4 at Jacksons Airport and what a mess I was, but I boarded the plane with a certain degree of optimism. Stan had told me how much he loved me and that we would be together again soon one way or t'other.

Dear friend Tony Holden and his family came down to the airport in Brisbane when I arrived, bearing flowers and gifts as a thank you for our friendship to him when he was based in New Guinea. They fussed over young Jane and as a proud new mother I found this charming. And Tonaks was there to greet me in Sydney.

In retrospect I was probably lucky not to have had more dramas over all those years. I was so careful initially but I probably became careless about my privacy. It was difficult to uphold the proven old standards when I lived so closely in bush camps. Because I felt I was partially to blame, I somewhat forgave the rapist/s in time but I went off sex for years and deliberately didn't accentuate by dress or behaviour; anything that made me look pretty or sexy.

I can remember the myriad of confused thoughts that passed through my head during that plane trip. I had learned a great deal having lived with so many dissimilar people in such unusual circumstances and was so much more astute than when I left Adelaide. I was apprehensive about how I could fit into southern conservatism not because of my New Guinea hang-ups but because superficiality no longer existed in my life and I had no idea nor cared what colour nail polish, or indeed what clothes designer was in fashion.

What I had learnt was to know, understand and respect the various nationalities and their cultures, so different to ours. I loved the New Guinea people and would miss them dreadfully but I had to wonder how long it would be before I wanted to return to that extraordinary lifestyle, if ever.

Of course, Stan had promised he would be down every few months and we would see more of each other than we had in the past! Did I believe him? Yes I did. We were wealthy now. New Guinea had been good to us and we had excellent people in management. I believed the business could be left safely in their hands when necessary.

As the plane circled over Adelaide on that day of my return in 1961, I felt strangely at peace. For the first time I think, I realised with pride that I was married to a great man. How he had survived and what he had accomplished in his lifetime was magnificent. Life without this brilliant, exciting, courageous, exasperating Polishman could not be contemplated. We were inexplicably bonded and a thought passed my mind that when I was quite old I would probably write about him and our life together. I was just 31 years of age.

16

A new adventure starts

The years raced by. Stan kept his word and initially came to us on a regular basis but with distance and time we grew apart. He was a great dad and he and Jane formed a close relationship. She had the advantage of travelling with her father overseas as a young girl and flew to New Guinea for school holidays. He was very proud of his intelligent daughter.

Stan and I remained close and never divorced. His final years were spent with a medical friend and following another stroke, he became virtually helpless but still enjoyed a glass of wine with friends. He died in the year 2000 and his graciousness and charm moved us all as on his deathbed, he offered the hospital sandwiches as if they were his beloved caviar.

Who could have guessed the twist in the story yet to come. Many years after leaving New Guinea I was holidaying in Broome. Standing on the tarmac waiting to take off on a tourist flight, I noticed a very handsome man with a shock of white hair jumping out of the cockpit of a smart twin-engined aircraft. Our eyes met and he stopped in his tracks, stared at me and smiled, and then walked on.

With a shaking voice and shakier legs, I asked an attendant

who the man was and she said, 'He's a legend here; a millionaire businessman called Roy James. Flies here often, a good bloke.'

Absurdly agitated I rushed out of the hangar and into the main building where I heard a voice from the past say, 'You took your time. What kept you so long?'

As I looked into familiar laughing blue eyes, I remembered what it felt like to be eighteen and engaged. Groaning inwardly I thought, 'Here I go again, another adventure!'

And I could hardly wait.

Epilogue

In 1962 New Guinea nationals were legally permitted to drink alcohol and The University of Papua New Guinea was established and in 1964 the first parliament, the House of Assembly, met in Moresby: the first step to self-government.

On 22 September 1964 the House of Assembly rebuked the United Nations for meddling in the territory's affairs and clearly stated they had complete faith in Australia. A motion was passed which stated:

> 'We the elected representatives of the people of Papua-New Guinea, desire to convey to the Parliament of the Commonwealth of Australia, The Trusteeship Council and the General Assembly of the United Nations Organisation, the expressed wish of the people that they and they alone, be allowed to decide when the time is ripe for self-government in Papua-New Guinea and the form that such government will take ...'

Self-government came to Papua New Guinea on 1 December, 1973. Most of us, black and white, understood it was too early – we didn't even have a constitution. It was as though we Australians had offered the hand of friendship and then taken it away and we felt we were failing the New Guinea people. The majority of the

New Guinea people didn't want us to go. We had assisted in providing education, health, law and order and financial aid for PNG's future independence but the problems of welfare, housing, border crossings from West New Guinea, and stability in jobs were still to be resolved.

Gough Whitlam, the leader of the Australian Labor Opposition Party arrived in Port Moresby for a fifteen-day visit in December 1969. He had already told the Australian newspapers that he expected a Labor victory in the next election and that Papua New Guinea would be given independence on his election as Prime Minister.

He chose to speak only to the minority English-speaking young educated elite from Rabaul and the Mataungan Association (which was fiercely militant against white domination). John Kaputin, a Tolai in Rabaul who at that time was considered a radical activist, and the Bougainville people were the only ones who supported Whitlam. There was concern about Indonesian control of Irian Jaya (formerly West New Guinea) and that Australian aid would cease. The Chinese in Papua New Guinea were also uneasy about their future. They had truly contributed to the growth of New Guinea, giving back more than they took. Enough to say the country was frightened.

Everyone was unsettled by a series of politicians visiting. However, it must be acknowledged that the politicians had a growing fear of Australia being unfairly labelled as 'colonial master' and change was inevitable.

On a lighter note, a great story is still told of Whitlam's return at the end of 1970 when a Labor member of his entourage, noting the hostile atmosphere jokingly whispered, 'If they kill Gough, declare me leader immediately.'

Michael Somare, the leader of the Pangu Party, with the assistance of the newly elected Labor government in Australia, presided over the ceremonies of Independence Day and at 5.15 pm on 15 September 1975 the Australian flag was lowered. At 10.25 am on 16 September, the bird-of-paradise flag of the independent state of Papua New Guinea was raised on Independence Hill at Waigani, Port Moresby.

We knew there were troubled times ahead and had hoped America would intervene but unfortunately this didn't occur. However I don't think any of us foresaw the chaos that has occurred, the decadence and the decay. Today, stealing and violence is rife. Shantytowns, or alternatively prison-like compounds and homes, now mar many areas once known for their great beauty. Houses with barred windows and doors are surrounded by high fencing with remote-controlled gates. Concerned parents drive their children to school, as it is often too dangerous for them to walk. Two-car families are prey to the *raskols*, and there are curfews in some towns. Bougainville has been an absolute shambles but one can only hope that law and order will be restored.

I had a dear indigenous friend, Joseph Minji, staying with me a few weeks ago. He is a successful accountant in New Guinea. I asked him what he was going to do if things did not improve. He said, 'My family and I are proud to be New Guinea natives. We will return to our village which by law each member part owns, and go back to the old ways if necessary.'

History

A touch of history for you:

Originally named the Island of the Fuzzy-Hairs by the Portuguese from the Malay word Papuwah, it was then called New Guinea by the Dutch because it resembled Guinea in Africa. The Dutch took over the western region around the 19th century, the Germans the north-eastern and the British the south-eastern.

The German-ruled region came under Australian rule in 1914 as the Mandated Trust Territory of New Guinea. In 1921 the two terrotories including their islands were merged. Then in World War II Japan overran Papua New Guinea, retreating in 1945. New Ireland, New Britain, and Bougainville were still held by Japan until Hiroshima and Nagasaki were atom bombed. After World War II, Australia was again invited by the United Nations to administer the Teritory of Papua New Guinea.

The Dutch lost control to Indonesia in the 1963 and this section was then called Irian Jaya. Unfortunately the Indonesian government led by Sukarno was unstable. The Dutch were excellent colonisers and there had been massive growth but under Indonesian control the plantations were unattended, and the assets were stripped.

Papua New Guinea was never joined to South East Asia but about 6000 years ago it was joined to Australia so we share many species of plants and animals. It is only 100 miles of water away from Queensland.

Australia has continued to support Papua New Guinea at the rate of approximately A$300 million per year and hopefully our excellent relationship will continue.

The Government administers schools of basic education and matriculation high schools. There are many fee-paying, usually expensive, private schools. Even though most villagers are articulate there are limited opportunities for them.

Nearly all Papua New Guineans are Melanesian. Women traditionally take the responsibility for households gardening and animal care, and men are the hunters and traders and responsible for clearing of the bush.

Because women are so important in the production of wealth it has always been necessary for men to marry and polygamy is still practised.

The Wantok System was under control prior to independence, however since independence it has become nepotism. Wantok is the pidgin word for 'one talk' – people who speak your language, kin, clanspeople. It means wherever you are, your clanspeople have a responsibility to feed and accommodate you. If there is a tender, then the contract has to be given to a Wantok. So in the villages sharing the spoils evenly works out reasonably well. Unfortunately in business it can be classified as outright corruption.

Acknowledgements

I am grateful to:

S. Aster, *1939 the Making of the Second World War*, London: Andre Deutsch Ltd, 1973

R. C. Lukas, *Forgotten Holocaust*, Kentucky: University Press, 1986

A. Lipscomb, R. McKinnon, J. Murray, *Lonely Planet*, Melbourne: Lonely Planet Publication, 1998

M. and J. Mann, *New Guinea – This Beautiful World*, Tokyo: Kodansha International Pty Ltd, 1972

Thanks to:

Brian Prideaux, my best friend, lover and pillar of strength;

the five brilliant women with whom I was privileged to work: Diane Morris (in my opinion a woman ahead of her time) and Doctors Hildi Bune, Margaret Rugless/Dorsch, Olive Johnston and Pat Sprod. They set a high standard and encouraged me all the way.

Julia Beaven for her editing.

Michael Schapel, Stephanie McCarthy/Linehan and Graham Phillips for good advice.

Southern Amcal chemist staff, Blackwood, for their cheery smiles and patience with my constant jamming of the photocopier.

Dean Wardle: without his computer skills there would be no book.

Temples and Tuk Tuks

Travels in Cambodia

Lydia Laube

The dinner menu had the usual interesting items such as 'Soap' and 'A Fried Monk' not to mention 'Chicken Amok'. The waiter couldn't tell me what amok meant, but I tried it and it turned out to be, not a crazy chicken running around with a cleaver, but chicken pieces in a soup coloured a kind of caterpillar-innards green that was very tasty.

Lydia Laube discovers that Cambodia, a nation with a violent and horrific recent past, is also an ancient, beautiful country populated by friendly, generous people who like to ride motorbikes very fast around corners.

Preferring the more sedate pace of tuk tuks, Lydia chooses this mode of transport wherever she can while visiting Cambodia's magnificent temples, markets, beaches and mountains – and, of course, the killing fields.

Deciphering the menu is only part of the intrigue of this mysterious land only just now opening to tourists and travellers. Join Lydia, squashed into a taxi with nine or so others, for an unforgettable ride.

Lydia Laube's first book, *Behind the Veil: An Australian Nurse in Saudi Arabia* has sold 30,000 copies in Australia alone. *Temples and Tuk Tuks* is her sixth travel book, following *Behind the Veil*, *The Long Way Home*, *Bound for Vietnam*, *Slow Boat to Mongolia* and *Llama for Lunch*.

ISBN 1 86254 631 2

For more information visit www.wakefieldpress.com.au

Dune is four-letter word
Griselda Sprigg

with Rod Maclean

Griselda Sprigg, her husband, Reg, and children, Marg and Doug, were attempting the first motorised crossing of the Simpson Desert. Steep, slippery sand dunes stretched behind and before them forever. 'Dune is a four-letter word,' muttered Griselda, 'and so is bloody spinifex!'

Dune is a four-letter word describes the Spriggs' pioneering adventures – not only in the Simpson Desert but across the vast Australian outback, as the family joined Reg in his relentless geological explorations. Griselda Sprigg tells a story of true love, a heart-warming tale of a family working together, and a humorous, earthy yarn about the bush and its characters.

Griselda's book is also the story of a great Australian outback resort, Arkaroola, and of how the Spriggs turned a drought-stricken sheep station into the magnificent flora and fauna sanctuary it is today.

ISBN 1 86254 540 5

For more information visit www.wakefieldpress.com.au

Wakefield Press is an independent publishing and
distribution company based in Adelaide, South Australia.
We love good stories and publish beautiful books.
To see our full range of titles, please visit our website at
www.wakefieldpress.com.au.

Wakefield Press thanks Fox Creek Wines
and Arts South Australia for their support.